Contents

Introduction 7

Chapter 1   What is Eczema? 11

Chapter 2   Who Develops Eczema? 19

Chapter 3   Symptoms and Diagnosis 27

Chapter 4   Different Types of Eczema 33

Chapter 5   Caring for Your Skin 43

Chapter 6   Treating Eczema 51

Chapter 7   Eliminating Triggers 71

Chapter 8   Caring for a Child with Eczema 79

Chapter 9   Complications 95

Chapter 10   Living with Eczema 103

Help List   115

References   117

Book List   119

For Matthew

Introduction

The purpose of this book is to provide information and advice for those diagnosed with the skin condition eczema. Whether you are a parent of a child diagnosed with eczema or have symptoms yourself, this practical guide will provide you with all the facts and resources you need to learn about the condition, the effects on your health and how to cope day to day.

Living with eczema can be challenging and it can have a significant impact on the sufferer and their family. If you have eczema or care for a child with it then you will be aware of how distressing and how demanding living with the condition is. Understanding the condition is the first step towards taking control of it.

In learning about the triggers and the treatment, you will be equipped to deal with flare-ups and to cope better when they occur. Knowledge and understanding are essential if you are to learn to control and manage the condition. Often time-pressed GPs diagnose and prescribe without explaining or helping their patients to understand how best they can help themselves.

This book aims to help you broaden your knowledge of eczema and its treatment, to help you communicate your concerns with your GP or dermatologist, and to identify a treatment strategy designed for your individual needs. In this book you will find information about the different types of eczema, treatment and management, along with practical advice and guidance on how to live with the condition.

The more you know about your skin condition or your child's, the easier it will be for you to keep it under control, to deal with treatment and to avoid flare-ups.

The challenge is to learn to manage your eczema and to not let it dominate your life.

Eczema can affect your psychological and emotional health, especially if not treated and controlled properly. Many sufferers find that they play down their condition; they try to put up with it simply because they feel that they have no choice.

'The challenge is to learn to manage your eczema and to not let it dominate your life.'

GPs can be complacent about treating it. They see many cases of eczema and often have only a 10-minute appointment slot in which to diagnose and discuss treatment options. But with such a complex regime of skincare management and treatment required, many sufferers find that they leave the surgery with a prescription and little knowledge or advice.

It can affect all areas of your life: childhood, school, work, sleep, social life and relationships, wellbeing and exercise. If you know how to treat your eczema and understand the flare-up triggers, then you can hopefully manage the condition successfully.

If you are the parent of a child with eczema, you will need to help them to understand their condition and why they need to undertake the sometimes rigorous regime of bathing and creaming the skin.

In order to explain this to your child you must first be knowledgeable about it. To help your child cope with the condition, you need to understand why eczema occurs and how best to treat it. In learning about the condition you will be better able to explain it to others - your child, their friends and their teachers, and learn to accept the limitations it might create.

Furthermore, in understanding the condition you will be better able to discuss treatment options with your dermatologist.

There are many types of eczema but underlying them all is the desperate itch, redness and inflammation. While sometimes eczema merely presents as rough, dry skin, at the other end of the spectrum skin can be thickened, cracked, weeping and very painful, with the condition impacting on everyday life.

It is often said that genetically-induced eczema cannot be cured but that it can be effectively managed. The tendency to develop eczema is usually inherited, but not everyone develops it.

It can affect any age group and varies in severity. Successful treatment and management of the condition can also vary from person to person.

Managing the condition involves a regular routine of bathing with emollients and applying protective creams and treatment ointments, such as corticosteroid creams as prescribed by a GP. With careful medical care the effects of eczema can be soothed, managed and controlled.

As well as learning about how to cope with eczema, it is important to learn how to address other people's reactions to it. Self-image and self-esteem can be damaged by such a visible condition and in knowing how to address other people's glances or questions you will be better able to feel confident in your own skin. While it can be easy to allow your skin condition to dominate your life and to feel less confident because of it, you must remember that it is an increasingly common condition. You are not alone. Many people endure feelings of low self-worth and battle with the ongoing flare-ups.

If you are the parent of a child dealing with eczema this book will empower you with the knowledge and techniques to help your child understand the requirements of regular application of creams and ointments. Children need to learn to manage their condition and to be able to deal with the symptoms which can be severe.

This book is your starting point in learning to live with eczema.

Acknowledgements

Special thanks to Hywel C Williams MSc PhD FRCP Professor of Dermato-Epidemiology at Nottingham University Hospitals, Queen's Medical Centre and Dr James Clifford McMillan BSc FRCP Department of Dermatology, City Hospital, Belfast.

Disclaimer

This book is for general information only and not to be used as a means of diagnosis or treatment of the skin condition eczema. It is to be used in conjunction with medical advice and is in no way meant as a substitute. If you have a rash or skin condition which you suspect is eczema you should seek a proper medical diagnosis and follow the treatment advised by your doctor. This book is intended as a guide, to help you understand the condition and to learn more about how you can best manage the condition.

'You are not alone. Many people endure feelings of low self-worth and battle with the ongoing flare-ups.'

Chapter One

What is Eczema?

Defining eczema

Eczema can be a chronic skin condition characterised by irritated, dry and itchy skin which is prone to periods of acute flare-ups.

The term 'eczema' comes from the Greek phrase 'to bubble' or 'to boil over'. It is also referred to as 'dermatitis' which means inflammation of the skin.

Eczema is one of the most common chronic illnesses affecting children.

Characteristics of chronic illness typically include a progressive condition or disease, which often cannot be cured but can at best be managed. The term 'chronic' refers to the longevity of the condition not the severity.

While there are varying theories on the exact cause of eczema it is generally believed that the skin condition develops as a result of both genetic and environmental factors. Some people have a genetic tendency to develop eczema. This inherited tendency to develop eczema and other conditions, such as asthma and hay fever, is referred to as 'atopy'.

Research has also suggested that eczema can be the result of a genetically defective skin barrier with genetics and environmental factors both playing a part in its development.

'The term "eczema" comes from the Greek phrase "to bubble" or "to boil over".'

Is it eczema or dermatitis?

The terms 'eczema' and 'dermatitis' mean much the same: an inflammation of the skin. There are two main types of eczema:

Atopic eczema is believed to be caused by a problem from 'within' the body. If you have atopic eczema you have inherited a tendency for your skin to react in a certain way. Various parts of the skin tend to be aggravated and irritated during a 'flare-up' period with your skin tending to be dry and rough.

'Endogenous eczema occurs when internal factors that are usually unknown, precipitate the eczema.' www.patient.co.uk/doctor/Eczema-on-Hands-and-Feet.htm accessed 1st October 2010.

Contact dermatitis is exogenous and is caused by an external substance affecting the skin. When the skin comes into contact with an irritant, patches of inflammation occur. Usually, removing the irritant is enough to help the skin inflammation to recover. There are two forms of contact dermatitis: irritant contact dermatitis, which anyone can develop when exposed to irritants like soap and bleach or degreasing agents like cleaning products, and the less common allergic contact dermatitis where people develop a specific immune response to something relatively harmless coming into contact with the skin, such as nickel (in costume jewellery) or rubber (as in rubber washing-up gloves).

'Contact irritant dermatitis may result from any weak acid or alkali, including detergents, shampoos and cleaning materials. It may result from foodstuffs, oils and greases. These may affect the dorsum of the hand first, but prolonged use over months or years leads to involvement of the palms.' www.patient.co.uk/doctor/Eczema-on-Hands-and-Feet.htm accessed 1st October 2010.

Is eczema an allergy?

Eczema is not an allergy as is sometimes believed, but instead it is an endogenous condition which some people are genetically prone to develop. One of the most common types of eczema is an atopic condition. This means you have a genetic predisposition towards the development of hypersensitivity reactions against common environmental antigens, most commonly associated with asthma, hay fever or eczema. 'Atopic' refers to diseases that are hereditary and therefore tend to run in families and often occur together.

This is often referred to as the 'atopic triad'. The conditions often appear together in one person and are found in other family members. So even if another family member doesn't have eczema, they may have asthma or allergic rhinitis.

The atopic triad

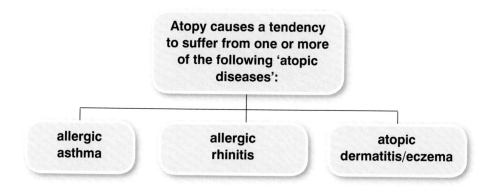

'Strictly speaking, to call somebody 'atopic' there has to be a demonstration of a certain type of allergic antibody (circulating IgE antibodies to common environmental allergens) in the blood. This can either be done by a blood test or skin prick tests and about 60% or 70% of the children with more severe eczema we see in the hospital are in fact "atopic". In the community where more milder cases are seen, it's probably more like 40% are atopic and 60% are not.' Professor Hywel Williams.

Asthma: When someone with asthma comes into contact with something that irritates their airways (an asthma trigger), the muscles around the walls of the airways tighten so that the airways become restricted and the lining of the airways becomes inflamed and starts to swell. It is not necessarily the case that one causes the other; the two conditions can co-exist and each does not always affect the other, although often patients can experience worsening asthma during a flare-up of eczema or vice versa.

Allergic rhinitis: This is a condition in which an allergen (something that causes an allergic reaction) makes the inside of the nose swell and become inflamed. This can cause cold-like symptoms, such as sneezing, itchiness and a blocked or runny nose. Hay fever is a type of allergic rhinitis that is caused by pollen.

Atopy is typically a more specific set of three associated conditions occurring in the same person, including eczema, allergies and asthma. Not every component has to be present at the same time, but usually these patients are prone to all of these three related conditions. This is why people often misunderstand eczema to be an allergy.

Eczema is used as a general term for many types of skin inflammation, characterised by fluid in the epidermis. There are different types of eczema, like allergic, contact, irritant and nummular eczema. Several other forms have very similar symptoms and signs. The diverse types of eczema are described in chapter 2.

Features of eczema

'Eczema is used as a general term for many types of skin inflammation, characterised by fluid in the epidermis.'

Signs and symptoms

People who suffer from eczema usually have dry, sensitive skin which is prone to inflammation. Having dry skin does not mean that you will develop eczema but people with 'eczematous' skin will usually have dry and often rough skin. The skin will appear dull and feel rough and scaly to the touch even in areas not directly affected by eczema.

Often eczema skin will be:

- Itchy, sometimes intensely so. The itch is a defining characteristic of eczema.

- Prone to rash: this is the inflammation. Scratching damages the skin cells and the body reacts by sending additional blood and immune cells to the area.

- Rough and scaly: the eczema-affected skin will be shedding and replacing dead skin cells at a greater rate than other skin. More dead skin cells will sit on the skin and this causes the scaly and flaky skin.

- Chapped and cracked: when the moisture escapes from the skin it dries out and cracks can form which are often painful and slow to heal.

- Blistering: vesicles, tiny clusters of fluid-filled blisters which are often itchy and when scratched burst and scab over.

- Weeping, crusting and scabbing: as a result of the scratched blisters.

- Painful at times, a burning-like sensation and the cracked skin can be very stingy.

- Feeling tight and restricted.

Skin affected by eczema will change, often starting out looking swollen, red and bumpy. When it becomes itchy it can also feel hot and painful. Little water blisters can also appear and when they are scratched they will burst and weep. The skin can then bleed easily if scratching continues and in the following days scabs will appear. When a patch of eczema clears up the skin is left looking dry, flaky, shiny and crinkled.

The itch is the most important symptom for diagnosis. It can vary from moderate to severe with significant disruption of everyday life. The characteristic eczema itch can be extremely distressing. Eczema can also be extremely painful.

How do I know I have it?

It is often said that eczema is easy to diagnose but difficult to treat. A diagnosis of eczema must be made by a GP or a dermatologist.

It usually begins in childhood but sufferers will experience 'flare-ups' - periods when the rash is more prevalent than others. We refer to eczema as being a chronic condition meaning that it will be a long-term problem. Acute episodes are when you experience a flare-up period, when certain areas or patches are particularly itchy, red and angry. This can lead to severe scratching and damaged skin, which becomes cracked, raw or weeping.

Identifying whether you have eczema

- Do you have itchy skin?

- Is your skin prone to red patches, particularly in skin creases?

- Is your skin dry or rough to the touch, almost like sandpaper?

- Is there a history of eczema in your family?

- Do you have a family history of atopic conditions, such as hay fever or asthma?

Although it can sometimes be triggered by an external agent, such as environmental toxins, internal conditions, such as poor nutrition and poor circulation, excessive production of mucus, food allergies and stress are also thought to be contributory factors to eczema.

Symptoms can range from dry skin to extreme itchiness which results in patches of bleeding, weeping and raw skin which crusts over and is at risk of infection.

Atopic eczema is the most common form of eczema and mainly affects children. While the exact cause of atopic eczema is unknown, it usually occurs in children who are prone to allergies.

A diagnosis is usually made by listening to the history of the rash - when it began and how it has appeared and felt, examining the skin and any patches present.

'Atopic eczema can't be cured, but there are lots of treatments. Patients must learn as much as possible and having access to good information is very important.' Dr Clifford McMillan. See chapter 10 for advice on using the Internet for research purposes.

Skin affected by atopic eczema reacts as if it is immune-suppressed. This means that it can be more readily infected by bacteria, viruses and fungi. Staphylococcus aureus infection of the skin is very common and frequently leads to small erosions, fissures, yellow crusting and scabs.

Summing Up

- Typically, eczema features include itchy, red skin that may be dry, thickened and painfully cracked. It usually affects the face, neck, elbows, hands and creases of the limbs, but can occur anywhere on the body.

- The appearance of eczema varies from person to person. In some sufferers small blisters form which are intensely itchy and when scratched, weep and scab over.

- The severe itchiness can result in the skin being scratched until the skin is damaged and at risk of infection.

Chapter Two

Who Develops Eczema?

Eczema affects males and females equally. Atopic eczema is more common in children, more common in families with a higher income and more common in wealthy countries, as opposed to developing countries, with north and western Europe seeing some of the highest rates of incidence.

Ethnically, white children and Asian children are equally affected, while there is some evidence to suggest that Afro-Caribbean children living in London do get more eczema than their white counterparts. (Source Professor Hywel Williams, Nottingham University Hospitals NHS Trust).

It is also more common in children from smaller families. Basically, while there is a strong genetic tendency, anyone can develop it.

'It is not all about genes, as environment is also very important indeed. The fact that eczema has increased in prevalence cannot be explained by genes, nor can the fact that eczema is more common in children coming from higher socio-economic backgrounds. Eczema is a so-called 'complex' disease resulting from an interaction between several genes and several environmental factors.' Professor Hywel Williams.

GPs are increasingly seeing more children with eczema. There has been a significant increase in the number of children diagnosed with the condition. Within a four-year period researchers reported a 42% increase in the number of cases. (Source Journal of the Royal Society of Medicine).

'The study found a 42% overall increase in the rate of new eczema cases each year. In absolute terms, this was an increase from about 10 cases per 1,000 in 2001 to 14 cases per 1,000 in 2005 (four new cases per 1,000 people over five years). www.nhs.uk/news/2009/03March/Pages/Eczemaontherise.aspx accessed 1st October 2010.

Atopic eczema affects about 15% of children and up to 5% of adults in the UK.

> 'It is not all about genes, as environment is also very important indeed.'
>
> Professor Hywell Williams.

'Approximately three in 10 people who visit their GP with a skin problem are diagnosed with atopic eczema.' www.nhs.uk/conditions/eczema-(atopic)/Pages/Introduction.aspx accessed 1st October 2010.

'In approximately 53% of young children with atopic eczema, it clears up by the time they reach 11, and in 65% of cases it clears up by the age of 16.' www.nhs.uk/conditions/eczema-(atopic)/Pages/Introduction.aspx accessed 1st October 2010.

Experts suggest that environmental factors are likely to be the main cause in the rise of eczema because it is highly unlikely that genetic factors would change in such a short time.

Most children's skin will clear up by their teenage years, though they often remain susceptible to it when the body is run down, under stress or subjected to irritants.

ScienceDaily (Jan. 8, 2008) - 'Experts are warning policy-makers that allergic disease might replace infectious disease as a major cause of ill health in cities undergoing rapid demographic changes in developing countries.'

It can be easy to underestimate the affect of eczema.

Case study

'My son is restricted in so many ways. Some days he limps because his ankles are so affected and the backs of his knees are raw so it affects how he walks. He is physically impaired because the skin can be so inflamed and when the scabbing comes he doesn't want to straighten the creased joints because it hurts so much.

'It is heartbreaking when the rash flares up and he can't straighten his arms because of the pain. His skin has even become thickened in areas where he scratches constantly.' JC.

How is it caused?

As we have discussed, eczema is not caused by one factor alone, instead it is thought to result from several factors which make people prone to developing it.

Some dermatologists have also identified what they term the 'barrier defect'. In other words, gaps in the skin that prevent sufficient 'waterproofing' of the skin. These gaps allow the skin to lose water too quickly. In skin affected by eczema the barrier is not efficient in holding moisture within and keeping microscopic bacteria out. This is thought to be the result of faulty genes.

Faulty genes also cause the immune system to be hyperactive in its response to an irritant. The hypersensitivity reaction leads to long-term inflammation. It often follows that if you suffer from allergies such as asthma or hay fever, then you will be more susceptible to eczema. There is some debate that the defective skin barrier gives rise to the secondary problems of food allergies, hay fever and asthma.

There is evidence of a strong genetic factor with family medical histories often showing several cases of eczema. Development of eczema is usually the result of several factors rather than just one easily identified and eradicated cause.

In addition, if you have a genetic tendency to develop allergies and are exposed to environmental triggers such as pollen, mould and fungi, mites and animal dander (tiny flakes of animal skin) then it is likely that you will suffer from eczema. However, some medics believe that the role of allergies has been over-emphasised since there are children with atopic eczema who do not necessarily have evidence of allergies.

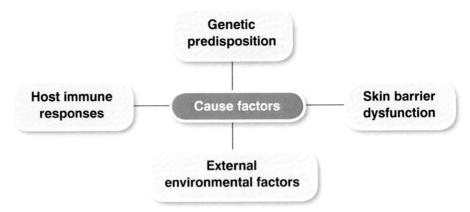

Inflammation of the skin refers to the reaction of blood cells and infection-fighting chemicals in your skin. The inflamed skin will be red, warm to the touch, irritated and swollen; which can also be itchy and painful.

Understanding your skin

Your skin is the largest organ of the body and it acts as a barrier to microorganisms and bacteria. It also provides waterproofing and regulates your body temperature.

The skin is made up of two main layers of cells: the outer epidermis and the inner dermis.

The outer epidermis is mostly made up of flat, scale-like cells called squamous cells, these skin cells, are constantly renewing. The flat, dead skin cells (keratinocytes) make up the main skin barrier, which keep moisture locked in and prevent harmful bacteria entering the bloodstream.

The other main layer of the skin is the dermis, the inner layer of skin which contains blood and lymph vessels, tissue fluid, hair follicles, and glands. These glands produce our sweat, which helps regulate body temperature, along with sebum, an oily substance that helps keep the skin from drying out. The dermis also contains the collagen and elastin which provide strength, flexibility and allow us to stretch. A layer of fat is found beneath the dermis.

'Your skin is the largest organ of the body and it acts as a barrier to microorganisms and bacteria. It also provides waterproofing and regulates your body temperature.'

What makes eczema skin so different?

Skin affected by eczema is different from non-eczema skin. The skin is supposed to act as a barrier, keeping irritants and infection out of the body. Research has shown that a flawed gene which fails to produce filaggrin (which normally pulls together protein filaments and flattens out dead cells to form the skin's outermost layer) is often found in people with eczema. It is believed that about one-third to half of all children and adults with moderate to severe chronic eczema have a non-functioning filaggrin gene, according to research carried out by Irwin McLean, a geneticist at the University of Dundee in Scotland, and Dr. Alan Irvine, a paediatric dermatologist at Our Lady's Hospital for Sick Children in Dublin, Ireland.

Eczema skin loses more moisture than non-eczema skin and as a result becomes over dry, cracked and prone to inflammation and allows irritants to pass through.

Myths about eczema

There are many misconceptions and myths surrounding eczema.

Does eczema cause scarring?

Eczema does not cause scarring although repeated scratching will cause lichenification - thickening of the skin and skin discolouration.

Is eczema caused by emotional problems?

It used to be accepted that eczema resulted from a response to emotional turmoil and while we know that stress can sometimes trigger a flare-up, psychological issues do not cause the condition to develop. Stress alone will not cause eczema. However, it is worth trying to reduce stress if you find that it does worsen your eczema or cause flare-up periods.

Is eczema contagious?

Part of the stigma of having eczema is that it is often wrongly considered to be contagious. It is not contagious. Eczema is not a disease you can catch. You develop it because you are genetically prone to it. You cannot catch it through touching it or by standing close to someone.

However, eczema sufferers are more likely to catch other people's infections. If you have eczema, it is particularly important to avoid contact with cold sores and impetigo.

Does the sun make my eczema worse?

No, not always. Many people find that the sun actually helps their eczema. The sun's ultraviolet radiation can help prevent the immune cells from causing inflammation. It is important to remember that too much exposure to the sun is dangerous and can cause skin cancer. It is best to always use sun cream protection. Some people find that their skin is too sensitive to be exposed to the sun and that the sun can worsen their eczema.

'Eczema is not a disease you can catch.'

You may find that on holiday your eczema flares up. This may be because of high temperatures making you sweat more, increased humidity and irritation from swimming pool water, as opposed to the sun alone.

A rare form of eczema called chronic actinic dermatitis that affects the face and neck of mainly middle-aged men is caused by a reaction to sunlight.

Is it caused by bad hygiene?

Eczema is not caused by poor hygiene. In fact eczema sufferers often need to bathe more often to help their skin. Furthermore, there is evidence that cleaner households are more likely to have a child with eczema.

The 'Hygiene Hypothesis' asserts that in modern life we have become too clean and that our children's immune systems are not exposed to enough germs to develop normally because of our use of antibacterial products.

David Strachan, an epidemiologist at the London School of Hygiene and Tropical Medicine, noted that children from large families were less likely to develop atopy largely because infections are likely to circulate more freely (BMJ, NOV 1989; 299: 1259-60). Up until this point it was largely believed that infections triggered allergies but the 'Hygiene Hypothesis' suggested that the immune system can be over-stimulated and this causes a reaction to allergens. It is too simplistic to say that we are now 'too clean' and that this has caused the rise in atopic conditions such as eczema. It is obsessive cleanliness that may give rise to an overactive immune system.

Summing Up

- Eczema can be a genetic condition and there is often a family history of it.

- One of the most common types of eczema is atopic dermatitis, also called 'atopic eczema'.

- The most effective way of keeping eczema under control is to practise good skin care and to avoid trigger factors.

- Eczema can affect all age groups. One in 12 adults and one in five children are affected in the UK.

- Living with eczema is challenging as it can cause emotional and physical effects, especially if it is not treated properly.

- Eczema skin loses more moisture than non-eczema skin and as a result becomes over dry, cracked and prone to inflammation and allows irritants to pass through.

Chapter Three

Symptoms and Diagnosis

Your diagnosis

Only a doctor or a skin specialist can diagnose eczema. It can be tempting to self-diagnose and treat your skin problem with over-the-counter moisturisers and topical corticosteroids, but for successful long-term care you need to have a proper medical diagnosis.

A diagnosis of eczema is usually obtained through a visit to the GP, although sometimes a referral to a dermatologist or a skin patch test is required when diagnosing contact allergic eczema.

An examination of the rash is usually sufficient to determine whether or not it is eczema. The doctor will make a diagnosis on the basis of the appearance of the skin, on the recurrence of the rash and a personal and family history.

'For successful long-term care you need to have a proper medical diagnosis.'

How will the doctor diagnose my condition?

The doctor will ask for a history of your symptoms; you should also think about what chemicals you could have exposed your skin to - from the mild cosmetics or detergents we all routinely use, to anything stronger - that you could have come into contact with. Consider your family history and if you suffer from other conditions, such as asthma or hay fever.

Each person can present with varying degrees of eczema and the GP will need to establish a picture of how the rash has presented. When it began was there an obvious trigger? How has it changed?

In some cases if there is doubt as to the skin condition, and to obtain a definite diagnosis, the GP may refer to a dermatologist. This would entail a small piece of the inflamed skin being removed and sent off for closer examination. Sometimes a skin patch test may be necessary to look for a reaction to specific allergenic chemicals.

Diagnosing a child with eczema

Being told that your child has eczema can be worrying, especially if you are told that it is a chronic condition which cannot be cured, although the majority of children will grow out of it.

Infantile eczema can appear from two months old, occasionally even earlier. It presents as dry, itchy inflammation of the skin, often appearing on the elbows, the creases of the knees, the wrists, the neck and sometimes the cheeks.

Every case of eczema varies and treatment needs to be appropriate to your child. Your GP will probably advise a combination of moisturisers, topical corticosteroid creams and ointments.

Sometimes the inflamed areas of skin become blistered and weepy and these areas are at risk of infection. If the skin becomes red and starts to ooze liquid, it may be infected, in which case see your GP immediately for antibiotic treatment. However, sometimes this could simply be the sign of an acute flare-up.

How can my eczema best be managed?

Sometimes the condition can be easily managed and under control while at other times, for no apparent reason, it can be exacerbated and flare up, disrupting everyday life.

Remember that eczema is subject to change and variation.

In order to understand the condition and how best to manage the symptoms, it is useful to ask your GP for as much information as possible. Sometimes it is difficult to know what to ask. If you have been diagnosed some time ago, remember that research has moved on and that there may be new treatments that you are unaware of.

It is important to develop a good relationship with your GP as routine follow-up appointments are necessary to successfully manage your condition.

Using diagnostic criteria

In making a diagnosis of eczema a GP will look for:

- Dryness of the skin.
- Itching, often intense and worse at night.
- Irritated skin with redness and inflammation.
- Areas of skin affected - elbows, behind the knees, the side of the neck or on the face of children.
- A pattern of flare-ups, periods of eczema activity which are worse than others.
- Family history of eczema, asthma, hay fever or food allergies.
- History of dry skin for up to 12 months.
- Secondary infection of the skin.

Knowing what to ask your GP

To get the most out of your diagnosis appointment you should consider what you need to know. Prepare some questions in advance.

- Can my eczema be controlled?
- Is the treatment risk-free? Should I be aware of side effects?
- How often should I use corticosteroids? What are the risks of using topical corticosteroids?
- What can I do to help prevent flare-ups?
- Should I be tested for allergies?
- Are there any dietary restrictions I should be aware of?
- What is the long-term prognosis?

- Are there any complications I should be aware of?

- How soon can I expect improvement?

- What kind of self-care measures can I take?

Fostering good communication

Communication with your GP is important since eczema is a long-term, chronic condition. You will need to see your GP for follow-up appointments to manage your condition.

'Ask questions; do not be afraid to voice your fears and concerns. Never feel that your question is too trivial – ask yourself, is this important to me or to my child?'

Listen to the information being given by the health professionals. Ask questions; do not be afraid to voice your fears and concerns. Never feel that your question is too trivial - ask yourself, is this important to me or to my child? The more information you gather on eczema the better able you will be in minimising flare-ups and implementing the treatment. Discuss treatment options, the benefits and side effects and what to expect.

Remember, the doctor is the expert. You are not expected to understand the condition overnight; there will be a period of learning about the condition and adapting to the treatment and if you have any queries then your GP will be the one to approach.

There are different types of eczema, each with different causes and varying symptoms. It is important to know which type of eczema you have in order to understand your condition and treat it accordingly. Ask your doctor if he can tell you which type of eczema you have. Atopic eczema is the most prevalent.

Most doctors are sympathetic and understand how the appearance of your skin can affect your confidence, how the constant itch can affect your everyday life and disturb your sleep, and how painful and upsetting the condition can be. If you feel your doctor does not appreciate how difficult it is to have eczema then you can always request a follow-up appointment with another doctor in your medical practice. It is important that your relationship with your doctor is good since you will rely on their advice and support in treating a condition which can affect you for many years.

'All doctors who are not skin specialists can underestimate atopic eczema. I often tell medical students that if they could experience 24 hours of bad atopic eczema then they would have a better understanding of what it is like to live with.' Dr Clifford McMillan.

Summing Up

- You need to have a proper medical diagnosis to ensure that you receive the correct treatment for your eczema.

- The doctor will make a diagnosis on the basis of the appearance of the skin, on the recurrence of the rash and a personal and family history.

- Diagnosing eczema is generally straightforward for a GP or a dermatologist, but identifying the actual cause or trigger of the eczema can be difficult.

- Treatment is often a matter of trial and error and working out what works best for your skin.

- Good communication with your GP or dermatologist is important.

- Eczema can be a long-term, chronic condition so you will need to see your GP for follow-up appointments to manage your condition over time.

Chapter Four

Different Types of Eczema

Eczema is also known as 'dermatitis'. 'Dermatitis' means 'inflammation of the skin'. There are many different forms of eczema and, as we have established, it can affect any age group or gender and its development and severity varies.

Atopic eczema

Atopic eczema is the most common form of eczema. It most commonly occurs in childhood, often before the first birthday.

While the exact cause of atopic eczema is unknown, it often occurs in people who are prone to allergies ('atopic' means 'sensitivity to allergens').

Atopic eczema is usually inherited and affects parts of the body where the skin creases, such as the backs of the knees and the front of the elbows, as well as the chest, face and neck. Men and women are affected equally. It can vary in severity with some people experiencing only mild symptoms, such as dry, itchy skin. For others the itch is intense and the skin can crack, bleed and scab over through repeated scratching.

Atopic eczema usually improves as the child becomes older and usually disappears in the teenage years. While there is no cure as such, usually the symptoms can be treated successfully and with careful management it can be kept under control.

'Eczema is also known as "dermatitis".'

Symptoms

The skin usually feels dry with some areas of the skin becoming red and inflamed. It often appears in skin creases, elbows and wrists, backs of knees and around the neck. However, any area of skin may be affected. The face is commonly affected in babies.

The inflamed skin is itchy and if it is scratched a lot it may cause patches of skin to become thickened. Sometimes the inflamed areas of skin become blistered and weepy and these areas are at risk of infection.

Allergic contact eczema

Allergic contact eczema develops as the result of a specific immune reaction to an environmental allergic reaction. The rash usually starts at the site of contact with the substance, but can spread to other areas. It is also known as 'contact dermatitis'.

'Contact dermatitis affects 9% of the UK population.'

Contact dermatitis affects 9% of the UK population and is the most common type of work-related skin disease (also known as occupational skin disease) since it can be a direct result of contact with a substance found in the work place. Significantly, if you had atopic eczema as a child, then you will have an increased risk of developing irritant contact dermatitis.

Allergic contact dermatitis is less common than irritant contact dermatitis. It is caused by a specific allergic reaction to a chemical following repeated exposure to the chemical over a period of time, often months or years. The body's defence mechanisms (the immune system) learn to recognise the chemical and the individual develops a reaction when the chemical contacts the skin again.

Symptoms

The rash usually appears at the point of contact with the allergen but can spread beyond. Symptoms can range from mildly dry skin to skin redness with the appearance of a burn. It can also be ulcerated with painful fluid-filled blisters. The reaction can be delayed depending on the type of allergen in question, sometimes taking up to 48 hours to have a full impact.

It is more commonly seen on the hands as they are in direct contact with the irritant. Symptoms are often red, dry skin which can become split, cracked, weeping and intensely itchy, sore, painful and stinging. The severity will depend upon the allergen and the length of time it is in contact with the skin.

Irritant contact eczema

Irritant contact eczema is similar to allergic contact eczema and is caused by frequent contact with everyday substances, such as detergents or cleaning products, damaging the barrier function of the skin. It is sometimes the result of years of exposure.

The irritants responsible are often detergents, cosmetics, and cold or even raw meat. While most people are aware of a reaction to strong chemicals found in certain work places, it can often be day-to-day exposure to cosmetics, shaving foam, bubble bath etc, which causes irritant contact eczema.

It occurs when the epidermis is damaged by an external irritant. Damage to the outer epidermal cells triggers an inflammatory reaction in the dermis and causes a reaction in the form of eczema. If exposure to the irritant is stopped then the skin will heal but if exposure is repeated and further damage occurs before healing has taken place, persistent eczema can develop.

'Irritant contact eczema is similar to allergic contact eczema and is caused by frequent contact with everyday substances such as detergents or cleaning products.'

Symptoms

Irritant contact eczema will often present on the hands, appearing as a dry, chapped rash between the fingers or under rings. It rarely blisters or weeps like other types of eczema unless it is a reaction to a particularly harsh chemical.

Seborrhoeic eczema

Adult seborrhoeic eczema is usually found on the scalp and begins as dandruff which then becomes red and irritated with increased scaling. This is when it becomes seborrhoeic eczema.

As the scalp becomes inflamed, the eczema may spread onto the face and neck and even the eyebrows, the temples, the folds at the sides of the nose and neck are sometimes affected. Seborrhoeic eczema can be particularly bad behind the ears with larger, greasy scales forming on the skin and surrounding hair, making the area look thickly crusted. The ear folds and ear canal may also be affected, causing irritation inside the ear which is called ear eczema.

Pityrosporum is a yeast which normally lives on the skin and is in part a significant factor in the causation of seborrhoeic eczema, although the exact mechanism for triggering the eczema is unknown. The greasy rash usually starts on the scalp as mild dandruff (sometimes called cradle cap in babies). The dandruff can get worse, causing redness and irritation on other areas of the body. Seborrhoeic eczema is common in babies under one, although about one in 20 adults aged from 18 to 40 also have it. It is less common in old age. Other areas which can be affected are the groin, the armpits, the breasts, between the buttocks and the genitals.

In babies it can occur in the nappy area and can spread to the face, neck and scalp.

Symptoms

When seborrhoeic eczema is mild the area looks red and sheds small white flakes of skin. The skin appears dry and flaky. In more severe cases it is very itchy. The scalp can be very oily, itchy and then inflamed with scaling forming. When it is on the face, the sides of the nose, the outer ends of the mouth and the forehead can be affected. The eyebrows are also prone to flakiness. When it occurs in skin folds, such as under the breasts or in the groin, the skin will be moist and red.

Discoid eczema

Discoid eczema can occur in adults at any age, but is more common in later life. It's often caused by dry skin becoming infected. It appears as disc-shaped patches of red, dry and itchy skin on any part of the body, particularly the lower legs.

Symptoms

The areas affected have a well-defined edge and will be red. They are often small discs of eczema with small blisters, scales or crusting.

Usually the pattern of skin lesions (affected areas) on the limbs is symmetrical. The lesions are very itchy which often leads to thickening of the skin (lichenification). Discoid eczema can often be mistaken for fungal infections of the skin, such as ringworm, because of the well-defined circular margins.

Eczema and the elderly

Eczema in older people is often overlooked, but as we have established it is a condition that can affect anyone at any age. While there has been an increase in eczema across all ages, eczema in the elderly is often neglected. It has been documented that up to 70% of older people experience skin problems and one of the most common of these problems is eczema.

Older people can develop eczema largely because of an inherent genetic tendency to eczema, along with such factors as sun damage and general poor health. In some cases older people find it difficult to wash and rinse their skin thoroughly and this can lead to skin irritation caused by detergents.

As we age our skin changes considerably. The natural oils in our skin deplete and changes occur in the fatty layer of the outer part of skin which maintains moisture.

'It has been documented that up to 70% of older people experience skin problems and one of the most common of these problems is eczema.'

Varicose eczema or gravitational eczema

Varicose eczema, also called stasis or gravitational eczema, affects the lower legs and develops more often in later life and is thought to be due to poor venous circulation. It presents as itchy and irritated, inflamed patches on the skin, commonly around the ankles. Recommended treatments are emollients and corticosteroid creams.

It occurs on the lower legs, over and around varicose veins and is associated with high venous blood pressure. Being overweight is also associated with the development of varicose eczema.

Symptoms

Like all eczema, it is prone to being itchy and red and will be found in the lower leg area.

If varicose eczema is left untreated and is severe, the skin can break down, with weeping, crusted areas which can quickly get bigger and become a varicose leg ulcer. A leg ulcer is a hole in the upper layer of the skin which can deepen and widen and become very sore. Leg ulcer wounds can easily become infected and can be difficult to heal, especially in the elderly as they often have poor circulation.

The first sign of varicose eczema is mild itchiness of the skin over and around varicose veins but it can occur when there are no obvious signs of varicose veins. This area will usually become speckled, scaly, inflamed and itchy and the skin can discolour, often becoming brown.

For some people, red inflammation occurs and it can be painful. Fibrosis in the skin may lead to tightening and narrowing. The medical term for this is 'lipodermatosclerosis'.

Causes of varicose eczema

Varicose eczema is caused by poor venous circulation in the legs and the general wear and tear of the delicate valves that stop blood from going back down into the legs again. These valves can become leaky, leading to large, dilated and varicose veins.

It often develops after varicose veins have formed for the following reason:

The valves in the veins in your legs weaken and fail to function properly. This allows blood in the surface veins to flow backwards. Surface veins become enlarged due to the backward flow. The pressure in the veins is also increased and leads to swelling in the nearby skin. So varicose eczema is partly due to increased pressure within the veins in the leg. The pressure builds up because valves in the veins fail to work.

Not everyone with varicose veins develops varicose eczema and it is not known why this is so.

As we know, scratching and rubbing at the skin will worsen eczema, while use of certain creams may cause further irritation. Many older people do not realise that they have eczema and fail to use the correct emollients or topical corticosteroids. The problem can escalate when ulcers develop which are more likely to occur in older people, since the circulation to the leg is poorer.

Treating varicose eczema

Treatment for varicose eczema involves good emollient therapy, topical corticosteroids and improving venous circulation and alleviating oedema (swelling).

Asteatotic eczema

Asteatotic eczema is also known as 'eczema craquelée' or 'winter eczema' and generally affects the over-sixties' age group. It appears on the lower legs, usually the shins and is cracked in appearance - like a dried-up river bed. These cracks can be red or pink in appearance. It often develops in those with a predisposition to rough or dry skin.

'Varicose eczema is caused by poor venous circulation in the legs and the general wear and tear of the delicate valves that stop blood from going back down into the legs again.'

The upper arms, the hands, lower back, trunk and thighs can also be affected. It usually appears in the winter months and affects more men than women.

Treatment

Asteatotic eczema is treated with emollient therapy and topical corticosteroids and it usually clears up, providing the causes are removed. Recurrences are common, especially in the winter months. Excessive use of soaps can cause asteatotic eczema and the use of 'water pills' (diuretics) is possibly a contributing factor in elderly people who may need diuretics to help correct a range of other medical conditions.

Summing Up

▪ There are different types of eczema with atopic eczema being the most common.

▪ Understanding the type you have is necessary in order to treat it correctly and effectively.

▪ Babies and children tend to have atopic eczema, which they can grow out of.

▪ Allergic contact eczema develops as the result of an environmental allergic reaction, whereas atopic eczema is an inherited condition.

▪ Eczema in older people is often overlooked.

Chapter Five

Caring for Your Skin

Goals of treatment

While atopic or endogenous eczema cannot be cured, it can be treated and the condition can be managed. Keeping your eczema under control and dealing with periods of inflammation is the long-term goal for treatment.

Looking after your skin

To manage and control your eczema you need to learn how to gauge your skin's needs on a regular basis.

You need to know how to care for your skin during good periods as well as during the bad ones. Looking after your skin when it is well can be difficult. It is easy to believe your eczema has gone away; that your skin is no longer in need of daily moisturising and special care when bathing. Don't be fooled. Keeping eczema at bay and under control can only be done through careful management and care.

Sometimes, even when you are following the recommended skincare programme, you will experience periods when for no apparent reason the skin becomes over dry and inflamed. Red, inflamed skin needs to be treated with anti-inflammatory treatments.

There are various treatments available and it may take time and effort to discover the best treatment to help your eczema. In its mildest form, eczema can be treated with moisturisers (emollients) and cold compresses to soothe the itch. In its most extreme form, eczema sometimes needs to be treated in a clinical setting with wet wraps, corticosteroids and antibiotics for infection.

'To manage and control your eczema you need to learn how to gauge your skin's needs on a regular basis.'

Treating eczema can be time-consuming and demanding, and when it subsides keeping it at bay also needs daily attention. Treatment requirements vary from day to day. It is a varying condition, subject to changing on an almost daily basis.

Learning to know what your skin needs

On a good day, you may only need to bathe and moisturise. On another day, your skin may feel particularly rough and dry so you will need to apply emollients more than once. Over time you will learn to 'read' your skin's needs and this will be an important step towards keeping your eczema under control.

Controlling and preventing flare-ups is an important aspect of your treatment. Many health professionals find that despite explaining treatment to patients many do not adhere to the advice fully and find themselves prone to flare-ups that are then difficult to manage. Part of the problem is that once the rash is under control it is easy to believe that it has gone, and then stop using emollients to moisturise the skin to help prevent inflammation.

Case study

'I think the key is to keep rotating the treatments - our chemist recommended this to me. Every six months or so, switch to one of the previous regimes and that seems to "fool" the system into submission.' DA.

Dry, itchy, cracked skin leads to inflammation. Moisturising helps to keep inflammation at bay. If skin is inflamed, you will need to step up your skincare routine to incorporate topical steroids which work as anti-inflammatory agents. Some people are wary of using corticosteroid treatments. But under guidance from your GP or dermatologist, corticosteroid creams can be used safely and can be most effective in treating the inflammation.

'If the skin is red and inflamed, emollients do not help very much. You must use an anti-inflammatory medication such as topical corticosteroids or topical calcineurin inhibitors (tacrolimus or pimecrolimus). The latter of course are only to be used for those who fail on topical corticosteroids, or in whom it is unsuitable according to the National Institute for Health and Clinical Excellence (NICE) recommendations.' Professor Hywel Williams.

Controlling the itch

Controlling the itch is an important facet of treatment, because when the skin is repeatedly scratched inflammation occurs, skin becomes damaged, the risk of infection increases and over time skin thickening and discolouration occurs. When skin is over-scratched it is vulnerable to outside allergens and irritants, which only exacerbates the itching.

Itch-rash cycle

The characteristic eczema itch is often said to be the worst thing about eczema. It is thought that people prone to eczema have heightened itch sensitivity. The itch is a built-in defense mechanism that alerts your body to the potential of being harmed. For instance, if an insect lands on your arm you instinctively itch and scratch. Receptors in the dermis become irritated and send signals to the brain. In people with eczema there can be confusion between pain and itch, with the signals from the nerves being misinterpreted so something which is painful can appear itchy.

Inevitably, itching will lead to scratching. Unfortunately, instead of satisfying the itch with scratching it has the reverse effect. Scratching will make the skin itchier because it damages the skin. This further damages the skin's protective barrier and makes the skin more susceptible to irritants. Itching also increases the release of more itch-inducing chemicals.

'The characteristic eczema itch is often said to be the worst thing about eczema.'

Immune system reacts to trigger

Inflammation occurs, redness appears along with itching

Scratching occurs which damages the skin causing further inflammation

Breaking the cycle is not easy but understanding that scratching worsens the condition and leads to further itching can help.

'Pain is easier to tolerate than itch. This is why people may scratch so much that they break the skin down causing it to ulcerate. It is because pain is easier to tolerate. Itch can drive a person to suicide.' Dr Clifford McMillan.

Breaking the habit

Since scratching is our natural response to an itch, we do it without thinking. Part of the problem of eczema is that the scratching damages the skin. All eczema sufferers experience an intense itch. It is a torment which can often only be assuaged through scratching. Eczema patients will readily tear at their skin, scrape it with sharp instruments, hair brushes, or even place their skin under hot water to try to take away the itch. They can leave their skin raw and bleeding following scratching.

Many patients will also pick at their eczema, rub at it and drag it over rough surfaces. All of these activities are scratching and they can all damage the skin. Do not fool yourself into thinking that by roughly rubbing or picking at your eczema that you are not scratching.

Become 'scratch aware'

Scratching can become a routine habit so much so that you can find yourself scratching unconsciously. To counteract the habit of scratching it is necessary to increase your awareness of when and where you scratch. You need to identify situations when you are less distracted from the itch and therefore more prone to scratching.

Some people find creating a 'scratch diary' is the best way to identify when they scratch. Jot down when you scratch and where. The only problem with this is that you may find you scratch so often that it is not practical to keep a written record.

In *The Eczema Solution*, Sue Armstrong-Brown (Vermilion 2002) suggests using a tally counter which is clicked every time you scratch. This gives you an idea of how often you scratch and encourages you to mentally take note of when you scratch, therefore making you conscious of it.

'You might also want to think about your scratching itself. How do you do it? Do you always scratch with your fingernails? Or do you have other favourite techniques? How do you feel when you are scratching? How do you feel afterwards? How do other people react when you scratch?' From *The Eczema Solution* by Sue Armstrong-Brown, published by Vermilion. Reprinted by permission of The Random House Group Ltd.

The urge to scratch is often worse at night as there are no distractions and the skin can be overheated. Keep the bedroom cool and dress in light cotton pyjamas. Use cotton sheets or a light duvet. Avoid close contact with pets prior to going to bed as animal dander can be a trigger.

Sometimes you might need antihistamines to help relieve the itch at night-time. Ask your GP if they would be appropriate to help you sleep and ease the itching at night.

'It is all well and good for me to tell a patient that they must not scratch, but the reality is that the itch can be unbearable.' Dr Clifford McMillan.

Behaviour modification therapy

Breaking the itch-scratch cycle is a significant factor in controlling eczema. Behaviour modification therapy aims to teach patients techniques that can help them avoid scratching. Patients also receive one-on-one advice and training, usually from a dermatology nurse, on how to incorporate their skincare routine into their daily life and how to best use moisturisers and their medications. Remember that treating eczema has to be multifaceted. There is no one solution.

Behaviour modification therapy is used in conjunction with conventional treatment. It is successful in that it can significantly reduce the damage caused by scratching and therefore limits the incidence of inflammation and subsequent infection. Anti-scratch suggestions include:

'You might also want to think about your scratching itself. How do you do it? Do you always scratch with your fingernails? Or do you have other favourite techniques?'

Sue Armstrong-Brown, *The Eczema Solution*, Random House Group Ltd

- Using a cold compress.
- Distraction techniques.
- Moisturising.
- Patting or tapping the skin.
- Keeping fingernails short.

While behaviour modification therapy is recognised as being helpful to some patients, not everyone will benefit. If atopic eczema is not scratched, it will not magically disappear. The problem will still exist but, yes, the skin will be less damaged and therefore less prone to infection and further flare-ups.

Case study

'The itch drove me to distraction. I constantly scratched, trying to find some relief. I would stand in front of an open fire as the heat would sometimes help alleviate the itch slightly on my legs, but most of the time I just scratched until my skin was raw and bleeding. Then the scabbing would start and that caused further itching. It was a vicious cycle which I couldn't break. I knew I was damaging my skin but I couldn't stop until I had torn my skin raw.' JMcB.

Developing a care plan

It is important to understand your treatment and to adhere to the advice of your health professional.

In discussing treatment options with your GP or dermatologist, you will be better able to understand the need for sticking to the recommended course of treatment and to care for your skin to help avoid inflammation and infections.

The variations of treatment can be confusing. Generally, creams are used to treat areas of skin which are weeping or moist while ointments are used on dry and thickened areas.

'Doctors need to spend time with newly diagnosed patients. Eczema can't be dealt with in one consultation. Dermatologists and GPs must allow them to come back with questions and have a follow-up appointment.' Dr Clifford McMillan.

Routine skincare

Successful management of eczema is firstly dependent on good skincare practice. Avoid soaps, bubble baths, perfumes or shower gels. Bathe in warm water with mild, non-drying emollient bathing lotion. When drying, pat the skin and do not rub. Then apply an emollient moisturising lotion.

Moisturising the skin can help to minimise the itching. Keep the skin supple by applying emollient throughout the day if your skin is dry and chapped. This is sometimes required up to five times a day.

How do I keep my skin moisturised?

The best way to moisturise dry, itchy skin is to 'soak and seal' - to bathe in warm water for up to 10 minutes using an emollient bathing lotion, not soap or bubble bath lotions. Then dry the skin gently, patting and not rubbing, and immediately apply an appropriate moisturiser to the still partly damp skin. Wearing loose, natural fibre clothing can help to prevent irritation. Remember, when your eczema is under control it is essential to maintain your skincare routine to avoid drying, chapping and flare-ups.

'The best way to moisturise dry, itchy skin is to "soak and seal".'

Summing Up

- To keep your eczema under control you need to develop a skincare programme which includes daily checking of the skin for signs of dryness or inflammation.

- Over time you will learn to 'read' your skin's needs and this will be an important step towards keeping your eczema under control.

- Do not assume that because your rash is under control that your eczema has gone away. You will be prone to flare-ups if you do not maintain your skincare programme.

- Make sure to bathe and moisturise with specially designed emollients.

- All eczema sufferers experience an intense itch; but scratching damages the skin, worsening inflammation and enabling infection to develop.

- Scratching can become a routine habit so much so that you can find yourself scratching unconsciously.

- To counteract the habit of scratching it is necessary to increase your awareness of when and where you scratch.

Chapter Six

Treating Eczema

Treatment options

Treatment for eczema needs to be multifaceted with the aim to calm inflammation, keep skin supple and moisturised, and to ultimately gain control of the condition.

There are many treatment options available and it is only through trying them that you will discover what works for your skin. Over time, you may find that treatment which has worked successfully will no longer keep inflammation at bay.

You must adapt your treatment accordingly. Try not to be disheartened when you still find flare-ups occur despite having maintained a good skincare routine. Inflammation can still occur when you are consistently moisturising.

Why does my treatment not always work?

Often treatment does not work, but the main reason for this lies in lack of compliance.

One common reason why treatment may not work is failure to continue using emollients that are part of your treatment.

Sometimes the treatment plan is not explained properly. Or the patient sees a result and stops further treatment. Treating eczema is challenging because it requires dedication, patience and time.

'I see people coming to my clinic with bags full of emollients and bath additives and no effective anti-inflammatory treatment for the skin of their child which is red and itchy and inflamed, the basic message needs to be reinforced time and time again, i.e. red and inflamed skin equals need for topical

'Try not to be disheartened when you still find flare-ups occur despite having maintained a good skincare routine.'

corticosteroids in short bursts. Emollients, of course, can be used on the same day as the topical corticosteroids but not simultaneously, otherwise the emollient simply dilutes the topical corticosteroid.' Professor Hywel Williams.

When the inflammation has recovered it is necessary to use emollients regularly in order to keep the skin from drying out and prevent further flare-ups.

Getting the most from your medical appointments

Be prepared; think about what you need to get out of an appointment and write down any questions you might have prior to the appointment.

Convey the full extent of your eczema; do not hold back on how bad it can be and on how bad it can make you feel. After all, the doctor is relying on what you tell them. Often by the time an appointment comes round you could be experiencing a good day so make sure they understand what it is like every day and on particularly bad days.

Do not feel obliged to take the information given without questioning it. If necessary, ask for a follow-up appointment to review your treatment.

Ask your dermatologist to provide you with a written treatment action plan. This should detail bathing routines, when and how to apply emollients and topical corticosteroid application when necessary.

Topical Treatments

A topical treatment is one which is applied to the skin rather than a medicine you consume internally. Treatment for eczema tends to be topical, with topical moisturisers and corticosteroids being widely prescribed and used in the treatment.

Emollients

Emollients are basically moisturisers and are essential in the treatment and management of eczema. They act by mimicking the barrier effect of surface lipids that are defective in eczema skin and increase hydration. When the skin is hydrated, softer and more supple, it reduces the need for further treatment in the form of corticosteroids.

Emollients can also be used to cleanse the skin and should be used instead of soaps, which can be extremely drying to the skin. Remember, not all emollients are suitable for your skin and it is often through trial and error that you will discover the one that works best for you.

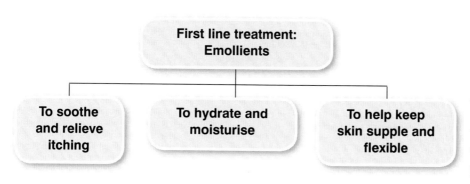

'Many moisturisers contain alcohol, which is drying to the skin, so it is worth checking the ingredients in the product that you are using.'

Many moisturisers contain alcohol, which is drying to the skin, so it is worth checking the ingredients in the product that you are using. Shop-bought cosmetic moisturisers can have ingredients which will cause adverse reactions and may make your eczema worse. It is often through trial and error that a good moisturiser is found and, remember, what suits your skin will not necessarily suit someone else's, and that your skin's needs can change.

While emollients help to soften and moisturise your skin, they are also providing a barrier to external irritants and allergens. They are important in treating and caring for your skin as they replenish skin moisture which is lost in skin cells in eczema sufferers. Basically, emollients soothe aggravated skin and protect it.

The most effective way of retaining skin moisture is to apply an emollient following a warm bath or shower while the skin is still damp. Use clean hands when applying creams to prevent bacterial infection. Pump dispensers are more hygienic than tubs of cream.

Even when you are experiencing a good period, it is important to use an emollient at least once daily. Emollients can be used as lotions, in bathing or as an ointment or cream. They can come in the form of aqueous cream and emulsifying ointment.

How much is enough?

Ensure you order sufficient amounts of emollient. It can seem excessive to go to your doctor or pharmacist with a large request, but generally you will need 250g per week for a child and 500g per week for an adult.

'Moisturisers are also very important in eczema. They come into their own for when the inflammation has subsided, i.e. to keep the dry skin, so typical of eczema sufferers, moist and supple. Emollients might also help the barrier function of the skin. Emollients can also be used as soap substitutes, as conventional soap tends to irritate the skin of people with eczema.' Professor Hywel Williams.

Which type is best?

Emollients come in three main forms which differ in their consistency:

- Ointment - provides a 'lock-in' protective layer to keep moisture from evaporating. Suitable if skin is extremely dry or cracked. Can leave a greasy film and can look unsightly so many people prefer to use it at night-time.

- Cream - is thinner in consistency and is easier to apply and leaves a less obvious residue but will be less effective than an ointment. Some people prefer to use a cream but accept that they may need to apply it more frequently than an ointment. Creams can be more helpful in treating acute weeping eczema.

- Lotion - has a runny consistency and will be less effective than ointment or a cream.

Generally, the rougher and drier the skin is, the thicker the emollient needs to be. Very dry skin requires an ointment, a cream for a more moderate spell or a lotion for periods when the skin is better. You need to apply your moisturiser in gentle, sweeping motions, covering all areas with a sheen. Smooth on gently, in the direction of hair growth to avoid blocking the hair follicles.

Emollients also come in liquid forms for use in the bath or showering. It is often a matter of experimenting and finding out which form and which product works best for your skin. Sometimes the emollient you use on your face will differ from the one you like to use on your legs, torso or hands. Discuss your emollient needs with your GP who will prescribe what is required.

Inexpensive moisturisers are often as effective as expensive creams.

'You can't over-moisturise and there are no long-term safety issues with using emollients.' Dr Clifford McMillan.

Corticosteroids

Inflamed skin must be treated. Mild corticosteroids, such as hydrocortisone (eg Dioderm and Efcortelan), are effective in dealing with flare-ups of eczema on the face. The torso and the limbs often need a more moderate strength corticosteroid for mild eczema, while a more potent one would be required for severe eczema.

Steroids used to treat eczema come under the groups of substances or chemicals called 'corticosteroids', relating to the body's natural hormone cortisol.

Corticosteroid medicines are mainly used for their effect in controlling inflammation, and topical corticosteroids are applied to the skin for the treatment of various inflammatory skin disorders. They have anti-inflammatory properties which soothe and calm irritated and aggravated skin. They do this by reducing the blood flow in the skin and suppressing the infection-fighting white blood cells.

Corticosteroid creams applied to the body and face are called 'topical' steroids. They work by suppressing your body's inflammatory response. It is important to continue to use emollients during your period of corticosteroid creams, but not at the same time, to avoid diluting the corticosteroid cream.

'You can't over-moisturise and there are no long-term safety issues with using emollients.'

Dr Clifford McMillan.

Remember: treat dry, rough-feeling skin with emollients and red, itchy, inflamed skin with topical corticosteroids.

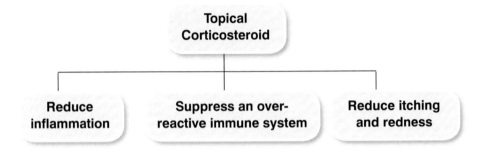

While corticosteroids are generally safe when used properly, they do have side effects so it is important to use them under your GP's advice.

How do corticosteroids work?

Corticosteroids imitate the effects of hormones which the body produces naturally in the adrenal glands.

When you apply topical corticosteroid cream to the skin, the corticosteroids are absorbed into the skin cells.

'They do cause local immunosuppression of course, but that's exactly what we want to do because the skin is over expressing immune reactivity.' Professor Hywel Williams.

These cells are then inhibited from producing various inflammation-causing chemicals that are normally released when the skin reacts to allergens or irritation. These inflammation-causing chemicals include prostaglandins and various other inflammatory substances. They cause blood vessels to widen and other inflammatory substances to arrive, resulting in the affected area of skin becoming red, swollen and itchy. By preventing these inflammatory chemicals from being released in the skin, corticosteroids reduce inflammation and relieve itchiness.

Are corticosteroids safe to use?

Like most medicines, corticosteroids have potential side effects and if not used correctly can have an adverse effect.

Localised side effects of topical corticosteroids include:

- Skin thinning (atrophy) and stretch marks.

- Easy bruising and tearing of the skin.

- Perioral dermatitis (rash around the mouth).

- Telangiectasia (prominence of small blood vessels).

- Increased susceptibility to skin infections.

- Allergy to the corticosteroid cream.

These side effects depend on the strength and length of time the corticosteroid cream has been used and the site of the treatment. Topical corticosteroids should be used only on the areas affected by eczema and are usually prescribed for use only once or twice daily.

'There is a lot of ignorance about topical corticosteroids and inappropriate fear of their use. Whilst it is true that strong topical corticosteroids cause skin thinning, we virtually never see such side effects these days when they are used properly.

'It is really important to be aware that some topical corticosteroids are stronger than others, and that where you put it on the body is also very important. For example, strong corticosteroids are virtually never used on the face, whereas they are the only thing that tends to shift troublesome eczema on thick parts of the skin, like the feet or hands.

'Similarly, length of application is important. Just dabbing some on every other day will not get you very far.' Professor Hywel Williams.

> 'There is a lot of ignorance about topical corticosteroids and inappropriate fear of their use.'
>
> Professor Hywell Williams.

Side effects

They can cause thinning of the skin, particularly on the face, which can make the blood vessels underneath appear more prominent.

Overuse can sometimes result in permanent stretch marks.

Fine blood vessels may swell and become prominent under the skin surface, causing a permanent change.

Sometimes the skin may become allergic to the corticosteroid, making the eczema appear to get worse.

A systemic side effect is one that occurs within the body. If used on large areas of skin for prolonged periods of time, potent corticosteroids can be absorbed into the bloodstream and affect other areas of the body. This is rare but it can cause side effects such as suppressed growth or adrenal suppression.

If too much topical corticosteroid is absorbed into the body it can suppress the natural corticosteroid production, which can lead to an illness called Cushing's syndrome. Children who need frequent or prolonged courses of potent corticosteroids are at a higher risk of these side effects than adults. Children being treated for severe eczema should be referred to a dermatologist who should monitor their growth and development.

Prescribing corticosteroids

They come in different strengths and are prescribed according to the severity of the rash with doctors opting for the use of the mildest dose possible to avoid side effects. If there is no improvement after three to seven days then a stronger topical corticosteroid cream may be prescribed.

The aim of using corticosteroid creams is to deal with a flare-up and to stop use as soon as possible. The occurrence of flare-ups and the severity varies from person to person and therefore your need for a corticosteroid cream will depend on the severity of your eczema.

Aim for the weakest strength possible for as short a time as possible, but if your eczema is severe or persistent and inflammation is heightened, then you may need a stronger corticosteroid cream.

'For acute flare-ups you have to use corticosteroids and doctors weigh up the benefit of using a stronger topical corticosteroid in short, sharp bursts or a mild corticosteroid for a greater period of time. Each individual case must be considered.' Dr Clifford McMillan.

How much should I use?

It is important to always read the information leaflet accompanying your corticosteroid cream and to adhere to the amount or dosage prescribed by your GP. The 'fingertip unit' is a term used by CC Long and AY Finlay to described a convenient way to measure how much cream to prescribe to a patient with skin disease. (Long CC, Finlay AY; The fingertip unit - a new practical measure. Clin Exp Dermatol. 1991 Nov.)

A fingertip unit (FTU) is the amount of ointment expressed from a tube with a 5mm diameter nozzle and applied from the first skin crease to the tip of the index finger.

'A fingertip unit (FTU) is the amount of ointment expressed from a tube with a 5mm diameter nozzle and applied from the first skin crease to the tip of the index finger.'

Area of skin to be treated (adults)	Size is roughly:	FTUs each dose (adults)
A hand and fingers (front and back)	About 2 adult hands	1 FTU
Front of chest and abdomen	About 14 adult hands	7 FTUs
Back and buttocks	About 14 adult hands	7 FTUs
Face and neck	About 5 adult hands	2.5 FTUs
An entire arm and hand	About 8 adult hands	4 FTUs
An entire leg and foot	About 16 adult hands	8 FTUs

Taken from http://www.patient.co.uk/health/Fingertip-Units-for-Topical-Steroids.htm and used with permission.

One FTU is enough to treat an area of skin twice the size of the flat of an adult's hand with the fingers together. When treating a child, one FTU is used to treat an area of skin equivalent to twice the size of the flat of an adult's hand with the fingers together.

Never continue use of corticosteroids beyond the prescribed time in the hope that it will prevent reoccurrence. Eczema will reoccur but constant use of corticosteroid cream is not a preventive cure.

'A once daily application is sufficient. There is no evidence that twice daily application (as often recommended in some of the texts) is any more effective and could end up giving rise to more side effects. It is also easier for families to manage and also cheaper for the NHS.' Professor Hywel Williams.

What happens if first-line treatments are not enough?

Emollients and mild corticosteroids are the first line of treatment for eczema but sometimes they are not always effective and a more intensive treatment programme is required.

There are a range of treatment options available but you will need to discuss your needs and expectations with your GP. It may be necessary to use stronger corticosteroid creams which are only available on prescription. Doctors often opt for the mildest form of treatment first and then respond with stronger treatment if necessary. If the inflammation is severe and not responding to topical corticosteroids the dermatologist can, in rare occasions, prescribe a short course of oral corticosteroids.

Prescription options

Stronger corticosteroid creams

Doctors do not prescribe oral or injected (known as systemic) forms of corticosteroids unless topical treatments have not worked. Side effects and risks of oral steroids are greater than topical steroids. Systemic corticosteroids work in the same way as natural cortisol. Oral corticosteroids, such as prednisolone, are available as tablets to treat severe eczema. They are used for the shortest period of time possible.

Immunosuppressant tablets, such as ciclosporin (eg Neoral or Sandimmune), can be prescribed for severe eczema. They can have significant side effects so are only prescribed with the lowest dose for the shortest period of time.

Topical immunosuppressants are creams or ointments that you apply to your skin to reduce inflammation. These non-corticosteroid immunosuppressants are part of a new group of medicines to treat eczema and are highly effective in suppressing the immune system and therefore dampening down inflammation and reducing the hypersensitivity of eczema skin. They may be prescribed if other treatments haven't worked or you can't use them due to side effects.

Antibiotics, such as flucloxacillin or erythromycin, will be prescribed if your skin becomes infected.

Antihistamine tablets that cause drowsiness can help you to sleep but they don't necessarily ease itching, although many patients report that they do help.

Weekend therapy

Sometimes a flare-up may respond well with topical corticosteroid treatment, but within a few weeks you might find that inflammation returns. If this happens, dermatologists sometimes suggest weekend therapy.

Weekend therapy typically refers to the application of topical corticosteroids for two consecutive days (usually on a weekend, but it doesn't have to be) in order to maintain control that has been gained through an initial burst of say 7-14 days. It tends to be used for more moderate to severe cases of eczema but is a useful way of maintaining long-term control without any fear of side effects because the topical steroids are only used two days per week.

This should be done under supervision of the GP or ideally a dermatologist in order to monitor quantities and to ensure adequate quantities are used to be effective.

Over time, weekend therapy can mean that the total amount of topical corticosteroid used is less than if each flare-up is treated separately.

Wet wrap treatment

In severe cases of eczema your health professional may prescribe wet wrap therapy. This is used when the first-line treatments of emollients and topical corticosteroids are not effective in dealing with a flare-up.

The skin is firstly 'soaked and sealed' - bathed and moisturised. Appropriate corticosteroid creams are applied and then the wet wrap bandaging treatment begins. Bandages or dressings are soaked in warm water and applied to the body and overlaid with a dry bandage wrapping. Sometimes gauze and surgical netting is used, especially when being placed on the face. Wet wrap therapy is occlusive dressing - it seals the inflamed skin from contact with air or bacteria and increases the concentration and absorption of the medication being applied.

The wraps help to replace moisture lost from the skin and help improve the effectiveness of the corticosteroid medication. Wet wrap therapy should only be used in severe case of eczema and under the advice of your GP or dermatologist.

NICE guidelines state: 'Wet wrap dressings, usually combined with topical corticosteroid preparations, can be very effective for short-term treatment of severe eczema.'

There are risks and any wet wrap therapy should only be carried out under your doctor's guidance.

While wet wraps can be effective, they are time-consuming and unpleasant. Most children will complain about having the bandages applied but as you become more used to applying them, the process will become quicker and the child will usually become more tolerant. The benefit of clearing up a stubborn flare-up will be worth the effort.

They are not an appropriate treatment if the skin is infected, as the warm, wet wraps would make infection worse and since prolonged flare-ups can indicate infection, it is essential that you consult your doctor before undertaking wet wrap therapy.

If wet wrap therapy is recommended for your child, allow them to practise bandaging their teddy or doll and help them to understand how the bandages will make their skin better. Apply the bandages while in a warm room, using warm water and place warm pyjamas over the top so that the child does not become too cold.

Case study

'My son's treatment needs to be so severe that he has been prescribed wet wraps. His treatment demands time and patience. Bathing him and applying the necessary corticosteroid cream and emollients and bandages is a nightmare. He has never become used to it and actively fights against the routine. It takes two of us, his dad and me, to apply his creams and it is upsetting for all of us. His brother and sister hate to see him so upset and I am constantly trying to make it up to him. Most nights he sobs and pushes us away. I feel like he hates me for enforcing the treatment.' JC.

Antihistamines

Antihistamines are sometimes prescribed to help alleviate the itch. They can be either sedating or non-sedating, although there is evidence that non-sedating antihistamines can also cause drowsiness. There is little research supporting the effectiveness of using antihistamines, but many doctors find that their patients do gain some relief in their use.

Antihistamines work by blocking histamine receptors, therefore reducing the reactions that cause itching. Histamine is a substance produced by the body as part of its natural defences and is released when the body reacts to a trigger, such as an allergen. However, histamine is only one of many substances in the body that cause itching and they mainly work because they cause sedation.

Sedating antihistamines are particularly useful at night if the itching causes disturbed sleep; they help to alleviate the itch while they also enable patients to sleep better. NICE recommends that clinical experience still supports the use of antihistamines in some situations, although this should not be routine.

Antihistamines can be given to children, though age limits do apply: hydroxyzine is not recommended for children under six months and promethazine and alimemazine are not recommended for children under two years. They should only be prescribed for short periods of time during flare-up episodes.

Topical calcineurin inhibitors

Topical calcineurin inhibitors, such as tacrolimus and pimecrolimus, are effective in reducing inflammation along with other signs and symptoms. These drugs are relatively new in the treatment of eczema but it is likely that they will eventually be used as part of routine atopic eczema treatment when further research has been carried out.

Topical tacrolimus (0.03%) is used for the face or mild eczema in those over the age of two when topical corticosteroids fail or are unsuitable, and the stronger preparation (0.1%) is used for more difficult eczema on the body. Pimecrolimus (5%) is used on any body site. 5% pimecrolimus and 0.03% tacrolimus are probably equivalent to a moderate potency topical steroid whereas the 0.1% tacrolimus is similar or possibly slightly less effective than a potent topical steroid.

The advantage of these newer preparations is that they do not cause skin thinning, but they are much more expensive and there are still some concerns about very long-term side effects with warnings that use of these medications may increase the risk of certain cancers, specifically skin cancer and non-Hodgkin's lymphoma. This is why they are only used at present when topical steroids fail. They are an alternative for patients who have experienced prolonged flare-ups which have become resistant to corticosteroids.

Phototherapy

Phototherapy exposes a patient to ultraviolet (UV) light for a controlled amount of time and may be prescribed to treat moderate to severe atopic eczema or contact eczema.

UV treatment for eczema can be a very effective treatment option. Phototherapy is often used as part of a total treatment plan which would typically include topical treatment along with trigger elimination.

Evidence has shown that UV light of certain wavelengths has an affect on the immune system. So, in creating exposure to these UV wavelengths for specified amounts of time, dermatologists are able to prevent the overreaction from the immune response that causes the inflammation.

Not everyone will benefit from phototherapy but for some patients the results are good.

Reasons why treatment doesn't work:

- The main reason treatment does not work is due to lack of consistency and too little topical corticosteroid being applied.

- Sometimes the skin is so inflamed that a stronger corticosteroid cream or a more intensive treatment programme is required to be effective.

- The dose of corticosteroid cream prescribed has been too low or the application has not been carried out correctly with the right amount being applied or because the treatment has stopped too soon.

- Infection could have set in and a corticosteroid cream containing antibiotics is required.

'UV treatment for eczema can be a very effective treatment option.'

What's the alternative?

Sometimes eczema flares up and your usual treatment appears to fail. This can be frustrating and upsetting. It is easy to feel disheartened when you are following your doctor's advice, only to find no improvement.

Each person's eczema and treatment differs. What works for one person may not work for another but there is much to be learnt from sharing information and comparing notes. There are no easy answers in treating eczema with either conventional or alternative medicine.

Complementary and alternative therapies

Complementary therapies are not generally recommended for eczema treatment and they are certainly not to be used instead of prescribed medication. If you decide to use complementary therapies then you should inform your doctor or dermatologist and seek their advice.

Be wary of anyone promising a miracle cure. Eczema cannot be cured by traditional or complementary or alternative medicine. It is a long-term, genetic disorder which will always affect you, sometimes appearing to go away completely only to return at another time.

Complementary medicines can help improve general wellbeing and help relieve stress which can exacerbate eczema.

There are herbal creams, supplements such as evening primrose oil, borage oil, homeopathy and Chinese herbal medicines on the market which aim to help eczema, but there is no scientific proof that they are effective or that they are completely safe. There are certain herbs and preparations which contain ingredients that can be harmful if not used correctly or if not obtained from reliable practitioners. It is important to research any complementary medicine thoroughly and to be aware of the risk of adverse effects especially with certain herbal medicines and problems of toxicity.

'Remember natural doesn't always equal safe.' Dr Clifford McMillan.

Dietary supplements, such as borage oil, evening primrose oil, vitamin B6 (pyridoxine), vitamin E and zinc, have been promoted as a safe and effective treatment for eczema yet there is a lack of conclusive proof.

Cardiospermum is a herb commonly used for skin problems in Sri Lanka. Its botanical term is 'Cardiospermum halicacabum' but is locally known as 'balloon vine' or 'love in a puff'. It can be used on the skin as a gel preparation which contains a tincture of the plant. The plant's main anti-inflammatory characteristics are found mostly in its leaves and seeds.

Manuka honey has been shown to have antibacterial, wound-healing and some anti-inflammatory properties. It can be purchased in a cream form.

Aloe vera can be soothing to red, sore and irritated skin. It comes in gel and cream forms and has some antibacterial and anti-inflammatory properties.

Oatmeal baths can be soothing and moisturising for eczema skin and have been used for treating skin conditions for thousands of years. To prepare an oatmeal bath you should place two cups of rolled oats in a blender, grind until fine and add to your warm bath water. Or alternatively place two cups of oats into a muslin bag and place in the warm bath water.

Using the Internet for research

The Internet is a rapidly growing source of information, some of it good and some of it not so good. It is necessary to ensure that the information you are accessing is from reputable organisations. Some information can be misleading and identifying the good from the bad can be challenging. (See the help list at the back of the book.) There are many sites on the Internet giving advice and information on eczema and treatment. Not all of these have the input or support from qualified sources. Be wary of information offering miracle cures.

'Eczema is very much a condition which requires self-help.'

Self-help

Successful management of eczema is dependent on more than adhering to the instructions on the label of your corticosteroid cream.

Eczema is very much a condition which requires self-help.

You need to have a good understanding of the disease, your treatment options and how you react during flare-ups. Altering your lifestyle to eliminate triggers and being active and healthy to avoid stress can help prevent flare-ups.

It can be easy to feel isolated because of your skin and to become depressed. One of the most effective ways of dealing with these feelings is to seek support. See our help list at the back of the book for organisations which offer information and support.

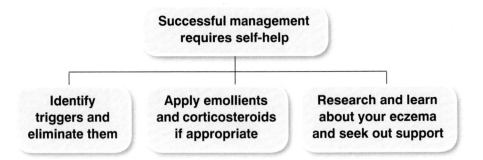

Summing Up

- Treatment for eczema tends to be topical with topical moisturisers and corticosteroids being widely prescribed and used in the treatment.

- Treat dry, rough-feeling skin with emollients and red, itchy, inflamed skin with topical corticosteroids.

- Emollients are more effective if applied following a warm bath, as this will make them more easily absorbed.

- Corticosteroid medicines are mainly used for controlling inflammation, and topical corticosteroids are applied to the skin for the treatment of various inflammatory skin disorders.

- Complementary medicines can help improve general wellbeing and help relieve stress which can exacerbate eczema, but they cannot cure it.

- Help yourself through learning about the condition and seeking out support.

P .

Chapter Seven

Eliminating Triggers

How can I help prevent flare-ups?

There are many ways in which you can help prevent your skin reaching the crisis point of inflammation. Identifying triggers - allergens which your skin reacts to - is an important aspect of managing your eczema.

The dry, itchy skin which characterises eczema makes it more prone and sensitive to irritation and flare-ups. Since those with eczema have a defective skin barrier, i.e. the skin does not sufficiently hold in moisture, when this factor is combined with irritation the skin reacts and becomes inflamed. The sufferer reacts to the itchy dryness by scratching and so begins a cycle of inflammation.

'Identifying triggers – allergens which your skin reacts to – is an important aspect of managing your eczema.'

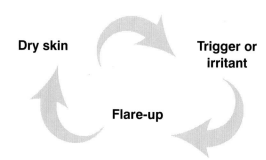

Dry skin

Trigger or irritant

Flare-up

Sometimes eczema can flare up for no apparent reason. Creating an environment in which your skin can be aggravation-free can really make a difference in preventing flare-ups. Learning to understand your skin's requirements and the potential triggers for your eczema is an important step in gaining control of the condition.

Allergens

Allergens cause the immune system to over-react and produce an allergic response and for some people this reaction becomes an eczema flare-up. These allergens might trigger a flare-up but they do not cause eczema; and so even if you remove all the potential triggers your eczema will still persist but avoidance of allergens can help.

It can be difficult to identify triggers. Sometimes dermatologists offer skin prick testing or patch testing to try to isolate certain allergies. This is probably only useful for severe cases of eczema and even then the skin can be so inflamed and the immune system so over-sensitised that the testing may result in false-positives.

'Some people find that over-tiredness causes them to flare, some people are worse in the heat, some are worse in the damp, some are worse in a dusty environment. So some form of avoidance or minimisation of such environmental stresses can be helpful. Using emollients regularly will also help to prevent flares as will wearing comfortable clothing, i.e. cotton and not wool.' Professor Hywel Williams.

Identifying triggers

We have discussed and explored the multifaceted approach to eczema treatment and highlighted that medical treatment is one aspect of eczema management. Skincare and limiting contact with trigger factors is as important. Medical treatment in the form of corticosteroids deals with the inflammation and infection but it is important to try to prevent skin from reaching this point.

Not everyone can identify triggers but for those who can, limiting contact with triggers or eliminating them altogether can have a positive effect in controlling eczema and helping to prevent flare-up episodes.

There are many triggers in everyday life and part of the challenge of caring for your skin lies in identifying the ones which you react to. If you can successfully identify them and then eliminate them, or at least limit your contact with them, then it can help lessen the incidence of flare-ups.

Toiletries and detergents

Cosmetics, toiletries, detergents and bathing products are all prone to drying out the skin and causing irritation. It is best to avoid products with artificial perfume and to use only hypoallergenic cosmetics. Be aware that companies can claim that their products are hypoallergenic without necessarily being beneficial or kind to your skin.

There is no evidence that non-biological products are gentler on eczema skin. Irritation is caused by residue left behind following washing with laundry products, such as detergents and fabric softeners. The best way to avoid this is by rinsing thoroughly and, if possible, setting your washing machine to do a double rinse.

Clothing

Many eczema sufferers find that rough fibres, such as wool, can annoy the skin. Smooth fibres and cotton are less irritating to the skin, especially in warm weather. It is often stated that cotton is better for eczema skin but this is only because of the smoothness of the fibres which make up cotton. Wool and polyester prickle the skin, cause itchiness and irritate it because they have shorter fibres which literally prickle and annoy the skin. Remember it is the texture of the fabric and not the actual type of fabric that is the trigger factor.

Temperature

Extremes of temperature and humidity can be a contributing factor in eczema flare-ups. If the weather is hot, wear loose, smooth fibre clothing, preferably cotton, to allow the skin to 'breathe'. Sweating can also make eczema worse as it contains chemicals which can cause irritation. A lukewarm shower can help, followed by your usual emollient to moisturise and soothe the skin.

Environmental

Irritants such as pollen, house dust mites, moulds or pet dander can be responsible for flare-ups. Your home can be a source of several eczema triggers - central heating, carpets, soft furnishings, animal dander and poor ventilation.

House dust mites can be a trigger for some people, with many atopic people testing positive to being allergic to them. To limit them in your home, it is advisable to dust regularly with a damp cloth and to wash pillows and duvets frequently in a hot wash. While it is impossible to completely eradicate dust mites, daily vacuuming of carpets does help to limit them. Make sure you do not empty vacuum cleaners in your house as dust mites will escape into the air causing irritation.

'Many atopic patients will test positive for house dust mites, but what does this mean? While one can reduce contamination it is impossible to eliminate them.' Dr Clifford McMillan.

Pets

Pet fur or hair can also be a trigger. They do not cause eczema per se, so do not feel that you have to banish them from your home completely. However, some people do have a specific allergy to animal dander - the flakes of skin which they shed - and it can cause flare-ups. Animals do contribute to the dust that builds up around the home, their skin sheds and their fur and hair cast, sometimes causing irritation.

If you suspect that your pet does trigger flare-ups or causes skin irritation, then make sure that they do not enter your bedroom and keep them from lying on sofas.

If you have a dog then wash it weekly and ensure cats are groomed regularly (make sure you do not brush animal hair inside your home).

You may find that you can tolerate the dander from your own pet but that another animal can cause problems.

'I would advise against getting a fur or feathered pet, but of course if the family already has one then the psychological damage of banishing a beloved animal would outweigh the benefits. If possible, keep a pet outdoors.' Dr Clifford McMillan.

Wellbeing

Some people, and especially children, experience flare-ups following viral illness. Being unwell may not be preventable but at least you can be prepared for a flare-up and treat your skin gently in advance.

Changes in hormone levels, for example during the menstrual cycle or pregnancy, can make eczema worse. While stress is not a cause of eczema, it is thought to be a contributing factor with many people experiencing flare-ups during stressful life events, such as bereavement or divorce.

'Changes in hormone levels, for example during the menstrual cycle or pregnancy, can make eczema worse.'

Controlling irritants

Wash clothes in mild detergents and double rinse if possible.

Avoid solvents, chlorine or known chemical triggers; if swimming shower well to remove chlorine and apply emollients straight away.

Develop and maintain a good bathing and skincare routine and do not use perfumed toiletries.

Keep house dust mites to a minimum through regularly cleaning and vacuuming.

Eczema and food

There is much debate about the role of food allergens and eczema. Some children with atopic eczema can be affected by food allergens. Allergens are substances that are foreign to the body and can cause the body to react in an abnormal manner by developing a specific immune response. This is known as an allergic reaction.

'Medical sources describe allergy as a hypersensitive tissue reaction to factors in the environment that for reasons not completely understood create special stress for that individual.' *Chronic Illness in Children Its Impact on Child and Family,* Georgia Travis 1976.

Even though some children can have atopic eczema and be affected by food allergens, childhood eczema is not caused by food allergy. It is unusual for atopic eczema in adults to be triggered by a reaction to a food.

Atopic eczema can sometimes be triggered or made worse by food allergens. The allergens cause inflammation-producing cells to react. Chemicals are released from these cells which cause itching and redness. The skin is then scratched in response to the itchiness and this damages the skin further.

Foods that might cause allergic reactions include:

- Cows' milk.
- Eggs.
- Nuts.
- Soya.
- Wheat.

Keeping a food diary is an effective way of trying to identify a particular food allergy, but it is usually best to do this under the guidance and supervision of a doctor. The aim is to identify a particular trigger food and then remove it from the diet. But often it is impossible to pinpoint a specific food allergy.

It has long been believed that milk and eggs are particularly the most common eczema trigger foods. However, a more recent study has found that babies diagnosed with atopic eczema early in life are at a higher risk of having peanut and other food allergies. The findings were part of a study presented by Graham Roberts MD, a paediatric allergist at King's College, London.

While there is some evidence of food acting as a trigger for eczema to develop in babies and young children, dietary restrictions are not always helpful. The exception of this is proven food allergies, such as egg or peanut.

Experimenting with dietary restrictions should only be carried out under supervision of a health professional.

Summing Up

- If possible, identify and then limit contact with potential triggers and irritants.

- Potential triggers can include: chemicals found in toiletries and detergents; irritants such as pollen, house dust mites, moulds or pet dander (tiny flakes of skin); being unwell, stressed or run down; changes in hormone levels - the menstrual cycle and pregnancy can make eczema worse; high or low temperature or humidity; rough fibres, such as wool.

- Learning to understand your skin's requirements and the potential triggers for your eczema is an important step in gaining control of the condition.

- Allergens might trigger a flare-up but they do not cause eczema and so even if you remove all the potential triggers your eczema will still persist.

- Even though some children can have atopic eczema and be affected by food allergens, childhood eczema is not caused by food allergy.

Chapter Eight

Caring for a Child with Eczema

Around one in five children will have atopic eczema. Parenting is physically and emotionally demanding, but when you are caring for a child with a chronic skin condition the demands are greater.

How eczema impacts on family life

It is clear that eczema impacts on the whole family affecting everyday life, holidays, social outings, meal times and sleep. There are everyday practical demands of caring for a child with eczema, as well as ongoing worry, stress and anxiety.

Caring for a child with eczema can be very difficult. You will experience helplessness, frustration and exhaustion as you deal with the demands placed upon you.

At times eczema will fade into the background of family life. You will all learn to live with it but during times of crisis and flare-ups there will be extra demands on your time and patience. Understanding the condition, developing a good skincare routine and being sympathetic will help you cope with the difficulties.

You will find that there will be:

- Daily demands of caring for the child's skin, maintaining a skincare routine and dealing with flare-ups and infections.

- Extra washing and rinsing of clothes, attention to providing a suitable diet, and dealing with potential triggers.

- Sleep disturbance and subsequent tiredness.

'Parenting is physically and emotionally demanding, but when you are caring for a child with a chronic skin condition the demands are greater.'

- Difficulties in coping with your child's behavioural problems should they arise.

- Problems in dealing with your child's issues of low self-esteem.

Will my child grow out of eczema?

You will undoubtedly be told that your child will most likely grow out of their condition, but ensuring that your child is able to cope with their present condition and adhere to their treatment is a big challenge. It can be frustrating to be told this, as if in the mean time you should just accept their eczema as a minor problem that will eventually just go away.

'Nearly all children with eczema improve, although only around 60% appear to be clear of eczema in teenage years,' according to Professor Hywel Williams. The reality is that even if their eczema does go away they will probably retain dry, rough and sensitive skin throughout their life.

Case study

'For me, the appearance of my skin was the worst aspect of eczema. I hated not being able to wear the same clothes as my friends, and had to cover up my legs and arms to hide the rash.

'When I came home from school I had to bathe in warm water just to ease my socks away from my legs as they would be stuck fast because of the weeping all day. It was painful and unpleasant.

'I lived with the constant hope that I would grow out of it. My family kept telling me I would and so I just wanted to be older for the rash to go away. When I was 21 it did subside and seemed to clear up overnight. Now I have dry, rough skin which is still sensitive. Since turning 21 I have had only one flare-up following the death of my mother.' JMcB.

Helping your child to cope

While working out a treatment plan and maintaining the daily skincare routine are essential aspects in treating eczema, so too is helping your child to cope with their condition.

Whether your child is three or 13, they will encounter challenges and it is your responsibility to help them deal with them.

On a positive note, there is much you can do to help your child. Talk to them about how they feel; don't assume that you know. If they are old enough to take some responsibility ask them how they want to manage their condition - do they want to apply their creams themselves or are they happy for you to continue doing so? Do they want to be reminded to apply their emollients or can you trust them to do it?

Share the knowledge you have gained in caring for them. Don't expect them to know as much as you do. Most GPs and dermatologists will have directed their conversation to you. Often children zone out and show no interest, but try to encourage them to be actively involved in appointments.

Explaining eczema to others

Children with eczema can have difficulties dealing with their skin condition, especially when they reach school age. The skin can look unsightly and attract unkind comments from other children who do not understand the condition.

Your child needs to be able to explain their condition, their treatment and how it affects them. It is a lack of understanding which causes problems. If your child encounters teasing or bullying they need to be able to feel confident in their ability to stand up for themselves or to approach a teacher for help. Providing your child with the knowledge to explain their condition will help them to deal with comments from others.

Through communication with peers and friends, the young person or child can encourage social inclusion and avoid feeling isolated.

When children are young they rely on their parents to communicate on their behalf but with the development of adolescence it becomes important for the young person to take responsibility for communicating their condition.

'Whether your child is three or 13, they will encounter challenges and it is your responsibility to help them deal with them.'

They need to develop skills to help them explain why they are limited by their condition, why they have the rash or attend outpatient appointments and why they require treatment.

For a young person to become confident in addressing these issues they need to have active involvement in their care. It is only when they have gained a good understanding of their condition that they can confidently address the questions raised by their friends.

Furthermore, your child needs to be recognised as being active in their care, which in itself will help give them some sense of control over their health management. Allow them to have some sense of control and responsibility and reward them for not scratching, helping to apply emollients and coping well.

Explaining eczema in child-friendly terms

Even the youngest of children can be educated about their illness, in age and developmental-appropriate terms. Knowledge eliminates fear and empowers your child in dealing with other people's questions or stares. Encourage them to ask questions about their skin and to learn all they can about their condition.

Sometimes role play is useful to help a child develop the communication skills required to address questions about their eczema.

- The rash shows that the skin is annoyed or irritated.
- Scratching makes the skin more aggravated and actually makes the itch worse.
- Eczema is not contagious, no one can catch it by sitting close to you or touching it.
- Eczema is not caused by a dirty home or a dirty child.
- It is not an allergy.

Working with your GP

If your child has a rash which you suspect is eczema then it is important to visit your GP and have a formal diagnosis. Seek professional guidance. You should not be tempted to diagnose and treat your child's skin condition without the expert opinion of your GP.

You may need to try different treatments and moisturisers to find the correct one for your child's skin. Do not use bath products unless they are emollients designed for skin affected by eczema. Bubble baths often dry the skin causing flare-ups.

Eczema is a long-term condition, so it is necessary to have an ongoing relationship with your GP. Ask your GP to help you learn as much as possible about eczema and to suggest reading material and helpful websites. (See our help list at the back of the book.)

The child will have a better chance of coping and ultimately co-operating and responding to treatment, if they too have an understanding of the illness. It can be easy to seek out information for yourself and not share it with your child, especially if they are very young when diagnosed.

It is important to know when to visit your GP. Following the initial diagnosis you may feel that there is nothing to be gained in making another appointment, but eczema is a long-term condition, subject to change and you will need to respond to those changes.

Visit your GP immediately if:

- The rash is severe and not responding to the normal recommended treatments.
- If a different rash occurs or the normal rash spreads.
- If the skin is particularly red, sore or weeping; and especially if your child has a fever.
- Be alert for signs of infection.

Psychological impact

There is evidence that eczema can have a psychological impact on children.

Ways in which the child can be affected:

- Sleep disturbance.
- Irritability.
- Behavioural problems.
- Low self-esteem.

Children living with eczema can often suffer from poor self-image, low self-esteem and little confidence. They understand that their rash can cause conflict between parents and disrupt family life, and this can have a huge impact on their feelings.

Trying to stop children from scratching can seem impossible.'

'Preschool children with atopic eczema have higher rates of behavioural difficulties and show greater fearfulness and dependency on their parents than unaffected children. For schoolchildren, problems include time away from school, impaired performance because of sleep deprivation, social restrictions, teasing and bullying. Psychological problems have been found to be twice those of normal schoolchildren among children attending outpatient dermatology clinics with moderate or severe eczema.' NICE Guidelines Dec 2007.

It has also been shown that atopic eczema can impair social development. The child can feel self-conscious; they are more irritable and difficult to parent. The sleep disturbance can affect the whole family and cause considerable distress. There is also some suggestion that mothers can find it difficult to discipline their child.

Scratching and children

One of the most annoying symptoms of eczema is the itch. Scratching is a natural response to the itch. Trying to stop children from scratching can seem impossible. It disrupts their sleep and can make them irritable and distressed. Over-scratching the skin can cause lichenification, damage the skin and cause bleeding and infection.

The itch-rash cycle results when scratching damages the skin and then we scratch again in response to the resulting inflammation.

Many children become compulsive scratchers and are deft at hiding their scratching. They use pens, toys and book corners; all sorts of objects to scratch at their skin. It is compulsive and sometimes even unconscious. Scratching can become a habit and your child can scratch without even realising they are doing so.

A major part of treating eczema lies in breaking the cycle of itching. To begin treating eczema and keeping it under control, it is necessary to help your child to understand why they must try to avoid scratching and encourage them to use their moisturisers as a way of relieving the itch.

If you see your child scratching, try to distract them, praise them for not scratching and even use a reward chart to help them resist the urge. Loose cotton clothes can help, along with keeping their nails short and avoiding overheating the home.

Case study

'Matthew must have his hands bandaged or wear gloves to stop him scratching at night. If we don't do this he tears at his skin in his sleep. He has never slept through the night because of the itching.

'Sometimes he must have his pyjamas changed in the night, as he often sweats and then the sweat makes his skin sting. When this happens I have to reapply all of his creams and start the whole bedtime routine over again.' JC.

Combating the itch

- Try soaking the skin in warm water and carrying out the 'soak and seal' method of moisturising.

- Avoid tight-fitting clothes or clothes with wool or polyester fibres.

- Don't overheat.

- Massage is an excellent way of distracting the itch and helping your child to relax.

- Teach your child to apply emollient when the itching starts.

- Wash and rinse new bed sheets and clothes before use, to avoid irritation.

- If you know your child will be sitting in the car for long journeys, encourage them to play with worry beads or stress balls to avoid idle hands scratching.

- Keep creams and lotions in the fridge so that they are cold when applied to the skin, as this can give immediate relief from itching.

- Keep fingernails trimmed and smooth.

- Try techniques such as blowing on the itchy skin or gently slapping or pinching the itchy area.

Helping your child to cope with treatment

Medics often report that the single biggest issue preventing successful management of eczema is failure to carry out prescribed medical treatment.

There are many factors as to why this occurs:

- Lack of understanding about prescribed corticosteroids and dosage.

- Failure to continue using emollients and moisturisers once skin has recovered.

- Difficulties in making children accept the need to apply creams.

Helping your child to accept and understand the need for treatment is one of the biggest challenges in parenting a child with eczema.

We have already looked at the importance of carrying out treatment as prescribed by your GP. It may be tiresome to follow the demands of a treatment programme, but the skin will improve if it is treated correctly over a period of time. There are no quick fixes but the results will mean that the whole family gain better sleep and general wellbeing.

The skin may look improved when inflammation calms down but the skin remains 'defective', dry and prone to inflammation so carry on using emollients, bathing in products designed for eczema and moisturising the skin.

When flare-ups occur the skin can be very painful, become cracked, weep fluid and bleed. Bathing may be difficult as the child may resist submerging the affected skin into water. Applying emollients and corticosteroid creams can also be difficult as the child may not want their skin touched and rubbed.

As with many illnesses, the most effective way of helping your child comply to treatment is to help them understand their condition and why they need to have treatment.

'A child can use eczema to control their parents. Treatment must be applied and carried out firmly but lovingly.' Clifford McMillan.

Enabling your child to take control of their eczema

Children from as young as three can begin to understand their condition if you explain it to them in age-appropriate language.

Encourage them to avoid scratching. Explain that the itch can be 'distracted' by cold compresses and that scratching will worsen the itch and damage the skin.

Explain why their skin is affected - tell them that their skin is not holding in the moisture it needs and that you have to help it by bathing and sealing in moisture with their emollient cream.

Help them to understand that their corticosteroid cream is 'medicine' and it will help to make the skin better.

Through better understanding the child will gradually take 'ownership' of their condition and hopefully work with you in treating it.

'A child can use eczema to control their parents. Treatment must be applied and carried out firmly but lovingly.'

Clifford McMillan.

Case study

'My eczema was diagnosed when I was just two months old. It was severe throughout my life and I had to be hospitalised twice and treated with wet wrap therapy. I was so young when I was diagnosed that I never actually had the condition explained to me. I just accepted it as I knew no different. Looking back, it would have been better if someone had told me why I had eczema and how I should deal with it.' JMcB.

Eczema and school

Children with eczema can face many challenges in the school environment, so ongoing personal contact with your child's teacher is important.

Your child's teacher may have a basic understanding of eczema but they may not understand fully how eczema can impact on your child's life. Sharing information about eczema will enable the teacher to be supportive. Unless they suffer from eczema, they will not understand the difficulties and problems which can arise from living with the condition.

Case study

'At school my son has struggled to reach his full potential because of his rash. He is constantly distracted by the itchiness. His teachers have been sympathetic but at a loss as to how to help him.

'If he doesn't want to do certain pieces of work his teacher has allowed him to sit with a book and not take part in the group. I know she is trying to be nice, but really I want him to learn with his classmates and not be given special exemption or excuses. It is difficult for me to push him knowing that he has to put up with so much and I guess the teacher feels the same.' JC

Topics to discuss with the teacher

Medical background, severity and occurrence of the condition, types of medication, frequency of flare-ups and any possible hospitalisations.

Sleep pattern and how your child's ability to concentrate may be impaired if they are waking in the night because of the itch.

Possible triggers in the classroom, warm radiators, paints, clay, sand and any other materials that could be used for play and learning activities.

Explain that while you want to avoid aggravating your child's eczema, you still want to ensure that they are included in as many activities as possible.

Discuss the use of special gloves to protect the hands during messy play or experiments.

If you feel that your child's educational needs are not being met or that issues of teasing or bullying are not being addressed, then you should request a meeting with the teacher and school principal. The school personnel and the parents need to work together to identify the barriers and be creative in finding solutions.

Often it is a lack of vision which prevents good educational support. Teachers may not have experience of working with a child with eczema and may not understand how they can best accommodate them. You need to be clear and emphatic about how distressing and distracting the itch can be. You also need to discuss the impact of the condition on your child's self-esteem and to ask the teacher to be mindful of teasing or bullying.

Concentration and the itch

Children with eczema can find it difficult to concentrate and sit still. This is a result of living with the sometimes intense itch. It is important to explain to your child's teacher that their skin condition can affect their ability to concentrate and that they are not being deliberately disruptive.

If your child has experienced a night of disturbed sleep due to their rash, then their ability to concentrate in school will be affected. You should inform the teacher if this has occurred so that they can be supportive during the day and accommodate your child's needs. Occasionally, you may need to allow

'Children with eczema can find it difficult to concentrate and sit still. It is important to explain this to your child's teacher and that they are not being deliberately disruptive.'

your child to sleep late following a particularly disturbed night and, with prior arrangement, you should be able to have permission for late attendance if this occurs.

Helping your child deal with eczema at school

Explain to your child that no one can 'catch' eczema, that it is not contagious and cannot spread even if touched by another person.

Explain to their teacher how the condition affects self-esteem and ask for their support and understanding.

Discuss how your child can best explain their illness to their peers. Teach them to be open and responsive to their friends' questions, but to not tolerate bullying or teasing.

Case study

'On one occasion, my son was on a school trip and another child didn't want to hold his hand because of the rash. My son was naturally very upset. The teacher stepped in and took his hand but I really felt sorry that he had to put up with this sort of prejudice.

'It has taken me a while to persuade him to take part in after school activities. He loves football but always wears long-sleeved tops to cover his eczema. Once, when the cracks on his hands began bleeding, the coach phoned me to take him home. I supposed he was concerned, but it was yet another time when Matthew felt excluded because of his rash.' JC.

Older children and school

As children progress through the school system they will have different challenges in dealing with their eczema.

PE

Physical education classes can be difficult if the child does not feel comfortable changing and showering in a communal setting. In some instances, particularly during flare-up periods, you may need to ask for your child to be excused from PE as sweat can exacerbate eczema and physical exercise can cause chaffing on sore skin.

Many teenagers are self-conscious about their skin and experience embarrassment when it comes to undressing.

Discuss changing room etiquette with the teacher and see if it would be possible for your child to change separately and to be given extra time to apply emollient cream following showering.

Case study

'The teen years were the hardest. It was so hard to deal with other people's reactions to my skin. I couldn't do PE because I didn't want to undress in the communal changing rooms or to deal with applying creams following showering.

'I was so self-conscious. My mother asked the school if I could be excluded from PE lessons and they agreed, but I really missed out on so much. I loved sport but no one thought to try to help me deal with my issues and to help me address the stares from the other pupils. They thought they were helping me by allowing me not to take part.' JMcB.

Some children and young people can deal with these issues without resorting to be separated from their peers, but not everyone is confident enough to deal with questions or stares. Help your child to be able to explain their condition and to deal with questions from their classmates confidently.

'The teen years were the hardest. It was so hard to deal with other people's reactions to my skin.'
JMcB.

Exams

Exam time can be challenging for everyone. For some people stress can be a factor in triggering flare-ups and the demands of sitting exams can take its toll. If your teenager is experiencing a flare-up, it will be almost impossible to sit through an exam without needing to scratch. The itch can be very distracting and can impair their concentration. It is necessary to discuss your child's eczema with the school well in advance of exams. The school needs to be supportive and to try to accommodate your child's needs.

It may be necessary to apply to the examination board for special dispensation, particularly if your child has eczema on their hands and has difficulty writing. Consider using a computer to complete the exam or having a special person assigned to write down the answers. Ask the school to help think of creative ways to ease the difficulties your child faces.

The child may need extra time to complete the exam. You should request that they sit in a cool room away from direct sunlight. If your child experiences a flare-up immediately prior to an exam and has disturbed sleep and impaired concentration, you can have a doctor's note sent to the examination board.

Remember, it is no use explaining your child's difficulties to the school after the exam has taken place. You need to keep the school informed from day one and for communication to be ongoing.

Summing Up

- Eczema impacts on all aspects of family life and involves: regular skincare treatment and applications of emollient, attention to providing a suitable diet and dealing with potential triggers, sleep disturbance and subsequent tiredness, behavioural problems, issues of low self-esteem.

- Children with eczema can have difficulties dealing with their skin condition, especially when they reach school age.

- Providing your child with the knowledge to explain their condition will help them to deal with comments from others and avoid potential problems. Helping your child to accept and understand the need for treatment is one of the biggest challenges in parenting a child with eczema.

- Medics often report that the single biggest issue preventing successful management of eczema is failure to carry out prescribed medical treatment, so aim to help your child understand their treatment and why it is important.

- Children with eczema can face many challenges when at school, so it is vital to have a good working relationship with your child's teacher.

- The school needs to know your child's medical background, severity and occurrence of the condition; types of medication, frequency of flare-ups and any possible hospitalisations; how regularly their sleep is disturbed and how your child's ability to concentrate may be impaired if they are waking in the night because of the itch.

- You will also need to make the school aware of possible triggers in the classroom: warm radiators, paints, clay, sand, and any other materials that could be used for play and learning activities.

Chapter Nine

Complications

Dealing with infections

Eczema is often complicated by bacterial, viral and fungal skin infections. When an eczema flare-up does not respond to consistent treatment, it is probable that the skin is infected. The defective skin barrier and the many fissures, or cracks, in skin affected by eczema make it more susceptible to infections.

These infections increase the severity of eczema, causing acute flares and secondary complications. Bacterial infections are more common in people and children with atopic eczema, though other types of eczema can also be affected by infections.

'As many as 90% of patients with eczema are colonised with Staphylococcal organisms.' Pediatric Infectious Disease Journal. 2008;27(6):551-552. 2008 Eczema and Infection Patricia A. Treadwell, MD.

Characteristics of infected eczema include:

- Hot, extremely itchy skin.
- Red, angry skin with weeping yellow or clear fluid.
- Pustules - yellow pus-filled spots.
- Yellow or golden coloured crusts.
- Swelling and inflammation or red streaks spreading from the infected site.
- Painful to touch.
- Enlarged lymph nodes (glands).

'Eczema is often complicated by bacterial, viral and fungal skin infections.'

- Failure to respond to treatment.
- Rapidly worsening eczema.
- Fever or malaise.

Staphylococcus aureus

The most common cause of infection in eczema results from a bacterium known as Staphylococcus aureus. Many healthy people carry these bacteria on their skin and in their noses without it causing any problems.

Infection occurs when during a flare-up period, the skin is scratched and damaged and the microorganisms are then able to enter the body through the tiny cracks.

'According to NICE up to 80% of children with atopic eczema are known to have Staphylococcus aureus, without obvious symptoms.'

Research has shown that Staphylococcus aureus is more commonly found on the skin of patients with atopic eczema than on the skin of people who do not have eczema. Research also suggests that people with atopic eczema cannot produce effective amounts of two natural antibiotic proteins that the immune system needs to fight infection. (Ong PY et al. "Endogenous antimicrobial peptides and skin infections in atopic dermatitis." New England Journal of Medicine. 2002. October 10;347(15):1151-60.)

According to NICE up to 80% of children with atopic eczema are known to have Staphylococcus aureus, without obvious symptoms. Everyone has bacteria on the skin; damaged skin enables the bacteria to enter the body.

Staph infection, as it is also known, makes eczema worse. If an infection is not treated the eczema will spread to other areas of the body not infected.

Children and young people with atopic eczema are especially at risk of developing skin infections caused by Staph bacteria.

If infection has been diagnosed then it is vital that you discard old supplies of emollients and creams as they can be contaminated by the bacteria and cause further infection. Your GP should prescribe new supplies of your regular medications.

If you have eczema, you have a higher chance of developing infection. Research has shown that because of the higher incidence of Staph infections, and possibly because of repeated antibiotic use to fight the infections, atopic eczema patients frequently develop MRSA infections (methicillin-resistant Staphylococcus aureus, which is a common skin bacterium that is resistant to a range of antibiotics).

(www.medicalnewstoday.com/articles/)

While we know those with eczema are more prone to developing infections, it is important to recognise the symptoms of infection as early as possible to seek medical advice and treatment. The seriousness and the longevity of the infection can be minimised if the infection is diagnosed and treated quickly.

Sometimes eczema can become worse even without physical signs of infection and it may be necessary to use oral antibiotics to deal with a flare-up which is not responding to consistent treatment.

Treatment for infection

If you have eczema and a secondary bacterial skin infection, you should treat it with specific antiseptics or antibiotics and topical corticosteroids, or other anti-inflammatory medications and moisturisers to repair the skin barrier may also be used. However, be aware that the corticosteroids dampen the body's immune system and potentially increase the problems of infection.

These can be applied topically as a cream, ointment or lotion. Studies have shown that topical antibiotics are successful in cases where pustules are present under the skin or when the skin is cracked, broken or weeping, giving easy access for bacterial infection.

According to the NICE guidelines, flucloxacillin should be used as the first-line treatment for bacterial infections in children with atopic eczema for both Staphylococcus aureus and Streptococcal infections. If a child is allergic to flucloxacillin then erythromycin should be used, with clarithromycin being used if erythromycin is not well tolerated, since it can cause nausea.

If the infected area does not respond to treatment, return to your GP and suggest that a swab is sent off for testing to ensure that the infection is not fungal and is being treated correctly.

'If the infection is very severe, oral antibiotics are essential; but if possible my preference is to treat infection with topical therapy.' Dr Clifford McMillan.

There is a lack of evidence to support the use of topical antibiotics to treat infected atopic eczema. Results from clinical trials that compared the use of topical antibiotic and corticosteroid combinations have shown no evidence that the addition of the antibiotic component provides benefit instead of using corticosteroid alone.

This does not mean that you will not be prescribed a topical antibiotic. Your GP may well decide to try a topical antibiotic if the infected area is small and localised. Long-term use is not recommended, as it can lead to the development of resistant bacteria.

If you find that there are particular areas of your eczema that are prone to infection, then a topical antiseptic may help. This is applied directly to the affected skin and works by helping to kill bacteria.

Bleach baths

Bleach baths have been used to treat eczema flare-ups and infection. The bleach is thought to kill the bacteria that grow on the skin which in turn reduces inflammation, redness and itching which prevents further scratching and helps break the itch-rash cycle. It is recommended that it is combined with other prescribed medications and emollients.

Some people, both adults and children, find that bleach baths are effective for dealing with infection and flare-ups, but others find that it causes further dryness and it can be painful if the skin is particularly cracked and raw.

The theory behind the use of bleach baths is that antimicrobial properties in the bleach combat the Staph bacteria and in doing so prevent the eczema worsening.

Bleach should never be applied directly to the skin, even in a diluted form. To carry out a bleach bath, add a small amount of household bleach - a half-cup of bleach per 40 gallons of water — and immerse the arms, legs and torso, leaving the neck and head above water, for five to 10 minutes each time. Pat dry afterward and apply a heavy layer of emollient moisturiser. Not all medics would support bleach baths and you should not undertake such treatment without consulting your dermatologist.

'I would be concerned that atopic skin is more easily irritated and bleach in a strong concentration can be corrosive. I believe the skin is too easily irritated to tolerate bleach baths and really an antiseptic or antibiotic is going to be just as effective.' Dr Clifford McMillan.

What can I do to prevent infection?

Staphylococcus aureus is found on the skin of the majority of people with atopic eczema, so preventing infection can be difficult. Looking after your skin and aiming to keep flare-ups at bay is the most effective way to avoid infection.

- Use emollients to keep the skin barrier replenished with moisture as frequently as possible. This will help prevent extreme dryness and cracks in the skin that allow bacteria to enter the body.

- Good hygiene is important; bathe daily and use pump-dispensing lotions and creams to avoid contamination. If infected, discard current creams and lotions to avoid cross-contamination.

- Try to break the itch-scratch cycle and keep fingernails short.

Keep indoor humidity and temperature the same all year round.

Avoid strong antiseptics as they can cause irritation and cause increased dryness and eczema to worsen.

'Looking after your skin and aiming to keep flare-ups at bay is the most effective way to avoid infection.'

Herpes simplex

Herpes simplex is the virus responsible for cold sores. If someone with atopic eczema is infected with the cold sore virus herpes simplex, they can develop the more serious condition called eczema herpeticum. They are especially at risk if they have not previously had a cold sore and have no immunity against it.

Herpes simplex often occurs in childhood. It is usually very mild, causing fluid-filled blisters which tingle, itch and sometimes are painful. It can occur around the mouth, on the fingers or on the genital area.

Eczema herpeticum develops as a group of small blisters which contain clear fluid or yellow pus. The blisters burst and ulcerate the skin. Once you have eczema herpeticum you will be prone to developing it again, and like cold sores you cannot catch it from someone a second time but instead it develops because it is already in your system. In someone without eczema, herpes simplex is found commonly around the lips. In atopic eczema sufferers it becomes more widespread.

Symptoms of eczema herpeticum

Eczema worsens despite consistent treatment and has painful areas of clustered blisters which feel like early-stage cold sores.

- Intensely itchy, but also sore.
- Fever, lethargy and feeling unwell.

It is vital that you see your GP if you suspect that you might have eczema herpeticum. In some cases, eczema herpeticum can be dangerous, with large areas of the body being affected and hospitalisation being required. Occasionally, it can be life-threatening. Treatment usually consists of oral anti-viral medication and can be started before diagnosis is confirmed following viral skin swabs.

Molluscum contagiosum

Molluscum contagiosum is caused by a virus and often looks like a series of small warts. It is common in children under the age of 10 and is caused by a pox virus. It presents as small, skin-coloured bumps which fill with material, turn red and then dry up and disappear. There are usually only a few of these spots and they usually clear up of their own accord. Children who have atopic eczema are more prone to catching molluscum contagiosum than those who don't.

Viral warts

Viral warts are common in school-age children. Again, if you have eczema then you will be more susceptible to warts. They are mainly found on the hands and feet (verrucas) but can spread to the face and lips. Unlike bacterial infections, they cannot be treated with antibiotics so it is often a matter of time for the immune system to deal with them or you can use treatments such as freezing.

Remember that medications prescribed to treat bacterial infections are not effective at treating viral infections.

Summing Up

- When an eczema flare-up does not respond to consistent treatment, it is likely that the skin is infected.

- The defective skin barrier and the many fissures, or cracks, in skin affected by eczema make it more susceptible to developing infections.

- Research has shown that Staphylococcus aureus is more commonly found on the skin of patients with atopic eczema than on the skin of people who do not have eczema.

- Children and young people with atopic eczema are especially at risk of developing skin infections caused by Staph bacteria.

- If someone with atopic eczema is infected with the cold sore virus herpes simplex, they can develop the more serious condition called eczema herpeticum.

- Children who have atopic eczema are more prone to catching molluscum contagiosum than those who don't, and scratching aids the spread of the virus into adjacent sites. They are also more susceptible to viral warts.

Chapter Ten

Living with Eczema

Eczema, as we have established, affects every aspect of your life. From childhood and school days, to adolescence, social life, work and retirement; eczema has an impact on how you feel about yourself and interact with others.

Caring for a child with eczema places the whole family under stress. The treatment, the constant battle to stop the scratching and the possible behavioural problems put everyone under pressure.

Case study

One mother describes her day:

'Our day begins with the same routine. In the morning Matthew's skin is often raw and bleeding where he has managed to tear at it in the night. I bathe him in special bath oil and apply his creams. His creams are applied at least three times a day, all over. The creams sting him and he becomes distressed. He becomes upset and I become stressed trying to comfort him while still needing to apply the cream. When the eczema is particularly bad he has to be creamed and then wrapped in gauze and bandages to stop him scratching at his skin.

'All of this while still looking after two more children, working and managing all the household tasks.'

Your emotional wellbeing

Eczema can take a toll on your emotional health. If you feel overwhelmed by negative thoughts, talk to your GP or dermatologist. Research has shown that eczema can cause depression, feelings of inadequacy, low self-esteem and behavioural problems in children. Seek ways of combating your low feelings, either through talking to understanding friends or going to counselling.

If you are a parent of a child with eczema your emotional health can also be compromised. The day-to-day demands of caring for a child with eczema can be wearying and at times you may feel depressed and despairing.

How to tackle stress and prevent depression

'Coping mechanisms can help you respond to the crisis periods and to live with the ongoing demands.'

It can be easy to feel stressed and to see no end to the demands of treating and dealing with eczema. Try to keep your emotions in perspective: it is a long-term condition but it is not life-threatening and there are treatments available.

It is well documented that chronic illnesses and conditions affect every aspect of life - the physical, the emotional, the social, and even the financial in that your choice of occupation may be determined by your eczema.

A long-term condition like eczema will often require adjustments in treatment and care plans. At times you may feel that your eczema is under control and then without warning it can reach an acute phase.

What are your coping mechanisms?

Coping mechanisms can help you respond to the crisis periods and to live with the ongoing demands.

We all have individual ways of coping with stress. For some, exercise is a positive response to feeling overwhelmed. You might enjoy listening to music or reading. Whatever your preferred way of relaxing and de-stressing is, try to incorporate time in your life to be able to unwind.

Understand that if you can relax and learn to de-stress you will cope with your condition better. If you care for a child with eczema, help them to identify a relaxation technique; or a hobby which can take their minds off their skin, the itch and the treatment. Remember, caring for a child with eczema is demanding so create a de-stress time for yourself as well.

You can employ problem-solving coping strategies

Research your eczema, learn as much as you can about treatment options and speak to other sufferers or supportive friends or family members.

It can be useful to identify your needs: emotional and practical demands. Discuss how your partner or family members can help you meet these needs:

- Help with picking up prescriptions.
- Reminders to apply creams.
- Simply being someone to listen when you feel low.

Write down what you want to achieve in your day. Don't allow it to become a list of chores, but instead think about things you want to do that will help alleviate stress - perhaps you want to have a quiet half an hour to read or go for a walk.

Encourage the family to exercise together. Sometimes just getting outdoors can help lift your mood and it will encourage the whole family to stay active, re-energise and feel refreshed.

Talk to someone who understands the demands of caring for a child with a chronic condition. Sometimes it helps just to be able to talk about the pressures and demands.

Seek out support from fellow sufferers.

The whole family

It is worth remembering that the whole family can be affected. Take time to evaluate how all family members are coping, especially well siblings. It can be easy to focus solely on the child with eczema and become wrapped up in their needs and concerns. The impact of a chronic condition like eczema can cause tension between siblings. Praise the well siblings when they are being supportive and understanding.

Talking about eczema and how it affects the whole family is the first step in dealing with the impact. Accept that eczema does cause changes to family routines and creates disruption, but try to make adjustments and work around obstacles to achieve a new normality.

How to include siblings

Explain how it feels to have eczema; tickle them with a feather and challenge them to not scratch. Now tell them to imagine feeling the worst type of itchiness all of the time along with tight, sore, cracked or raw skin.

Just being involved can help them to feel included and less overlooked. It will also help them appreciate the difficulties of living with eczema.

'Just being involved can help siblings to feel included and less overlooked.'

Ask for their help; older siblings can help apply emollients and a younger child can help bring a cream to their brother or sister. Ask them to help distract the eczema sufferer from itchiness.

Reward their support with outings, treats or just a hug of appreciation.

Easing the burden on family life

Try to instil a sense of working together to deal with the eczema. Encouraging responsibility for treatment will help the child or young person to accept their treatment and to cope better.

Develop a routine for ordering medicines and applying them. This will help to minimise the impact of the treatment on family life. Everyone will soon learn to adapt to the routine and understand when your attention will be on bathing and applying creams.

Try to create a calm atmosphere for applying creams, play soothing music or encourage the child to watch a favourite programme while you are applying creams to help distract and relax them.

Self-image

Eczema is more than a medical condition which affects the skin; it goes much deeper and affects self-image, confidence and self-esteem. It has an impact on our emotional health and needs to be recognised as being challenging to live with. All too often eczema is dismissed as a relatively minor ailment that children grow out of. Eczema is often a life-long condition which can affect children, teenagers, adults and the elderly.

Appearance and how we are seen by others can really affect our self-esteem. Many people with eczema talk about how they are embarrassed and ashamed of their skin condition and how it affects them socially. It can be difficult to make new friends or to form relationships if you are conscious of your skin.

How can you improve self-esteem?

Remember that while eczema can cause great discomfort and terrible distress, it is a relatively non-serious condition and that you will experience periods when the skin looks better and feels better.

It is not contagious so you cannot pass it on to others.

You are more than your skin; try to think of all the positive aspects of your personality, health and life that you can feel grateful for.

Don't let your eczema limit your life. Try to be creative and find ways around your eczema to do exactly what you want.

'Understanding the condition is the first step in taking control of it and learning to live with it.'

Creating a personal programme for living with eczema

You should now have a good understanding of what eczema is, how it affects everyday life and how it can be treated. Understanding the condition is the first step in taking control of it and learning to live with it.

Recognise your eczema for what it is: a chronic, recurring skin condition. It can be managed and you should aim to keep it under control.

Be realistic, know that you will experience periods when your skin is irritated and itchy, cracked and sore, but take action to deal with these periods.

Identify your treatment goals and accept your eczema as part of your life.

Treatment goals:

- Nourish your skin and replenish lost moisture.
- Deal with acute flare-ups.
- Respond to infection.

Routine care

Regularly check your skin for dryness, patches of eczema and signs of infection. Daily inspections first thing in the morning will help you to identify troublesome areas which you have perhaps scratched and damaged in your sleep. Scratched areas and broken skin need to be treated carefully to avoid infection.

To manage your condition you need to:

- Identify your particular type of eczema.
- Understand how it reacts to any triggers.
- Know how it is treated.
- Understand how to prevent flare-ups through a good skincare routine.

Tackling your eczema

- Keep a diary to help create a picture of flare-ups, how often they occur, how bad they are and what, if anything, triggers them.
- Develop and maintain a good skincare routine: bathe, pat dry, moisturise. Use emollients throughout the day.
- Avoid allowing the skin to become over dry.

- Wear lightweight, breathable and smooth fibre fabrics.

- Avoid extremes of temperature.

- Do not drink alcohol in excess and avoid smoky atmospheres.

- Keep an active interest in any new research or developments with regards to treatment. New emollient products and medicines come on to the market all the time and you may find one that works better for you.

Take control

- Become well-informed about eczema and how to treat it.

- Stay healthy and active. Eat well and try to deal effectively with stress.

- Maintain a good personal skincare routine.

Everyday life

Part of learning to cope with your eczema is incorporating it and the treatment into your everyday life. To help keep the rash under control and to eliminate potential triggers, there are some actions you can take around your home. Modifying your home and your lifestyle can be an important step in gaining control of your condition.

- Keep your room temperatures cool and use a humidifier if the atmosphere is particularly dry, while also keeping rooms well ventilated.

- Dust regularly with a damp cloth.

- Limit the number of carpets and rugs, to keep dust and house mites under control.

- Change bedding regularly, wash pillows and duvets and vacuum mattresses.

- Choose household cleaning products carefully, avoiding chemicals which can trigger your eczema.

- Use rubber gloves when cleaning and, if necessary, wear cotton gloves beneath them.

- Limit the spaces that pets can roam in and try to prevent them from sleeping on sofas and beds.

- Alcohol can lead to dehydration so drink sensibly to avoid flare-ups. Smoking or being in a smoky atmosphere can also irritate exposed skin.

Your daily care plan

To treat your eczema and to prevent flare-ups you need to be consistent and systematic in your approach.

Each morning examine your skin, looking for dry patches, scratched or damaged areas and signs of infection.

Shower or bathe using emollient washes, pat the skin dry and apply emollient cream or lotion to protect and repair.

If skin feels moderately dry moisturise twice a day - get into the habit of doing this when you brush your teeth or wash.

If your skin feels particularly dry, rough or itchy then be aware that you could be about to experience a flare-up. Ensure that your corticosteroid creams and emollients are up to date and within easy access throughout the day.

You can use a thicker cream if you feel your skin is very rough and dry and apply it up to four times a day. If it is easier, use a normal lotion throughout the day and apply a thicker cream at night-time after bathing.

For flare times use the 'soak and seal' method - bathe, pat dry and moisturise with a heavy, greasy cream before later applying your prescribed topical corticosteroid ointments to flare-up patches of inflammation.

Watch for signs of infection and seek medical advice if you suspect that your skin is infected.

Exercise and eczema

We all need to incorporate exercise into our lives to ensure we are healthy and fit. It is also a great stress-buster.

To ensure that exercise does not exacerbate your eczema, wear loose-fitting clothes, shower after exercise to avoid allowing sweat to irritate the skin and apply your usual emollient moisturisers.

If you like to swim, apply emollient before you enter the pool. The higher the level of chlorine in the water the greater the chances are of it causing irritation. Shower off as soon as you leave the pool and apply your emollients.

Work life and eczema

Your choice of occupation can have a significant impact on eczema. Working with chemicals, dust or sand can exacerbate eczema or cause conditions such as contact dermatitis. Your work environment can either directly cause eczema or worsen it by being a trigger for flare-ups.

Occupations which are potentially the most problematic are: floristry, hairdressing, manufacturing or factory work, beauty therapy and healthcare work (mainly nursing).

'Seek clean, dry work and avoid wet work and irritants.' Dr Clifford McMillan.

We know that the risk factors and common features of these jobs are frequent hand-washing or wet work, exposure to irritant and allergenic chemicals, along with frequent or persistent glove-wearing.

'Seek clean, dry work and avoid wet work and irritants.'
Dr Clifford McMillan.

Your rights and occupational eczema

Under employment law employees can expect employers to adequately control exposure to hazards in the workplace that cause ill health. This includes controlling exposure to substances that cause eczema.

You should notify your employer if you already know of any harm that substances you are working with can cause you. Your employer should investigate alternative working arrangements, whether that is exchanging one substance for another or possibly arranging for you to have the minimal amount of contact with the substance by using splash guards or extractors, for example.

Employers should also provide protective clothing to wear, such as gloves or overalls, which prevent the substance from coming into contact with your skin. Providing this protective clothing is made available to you, it is your responsibility as an employee to wear the clothing at all times and protect yourself.

If you develop eczema or dermatitis later on in life or if your condition significantly worsens later in life, then there is a chance that it could have been caused by your working conditions and you could be able to claim compensation.

Summing Up

- Research has shown that eczema can cause depression, feelings of inadequacy, low self-esteem and behavioural problems in children.

- Caring for a child with eczema places the whole family under stress.

- Research your eczema, learn as much as you can about treatment options and speak to other sufferers or supportive friends or family members.

- Recognise your eczema for what it is: a chronic, recurring skin condition.

Help List

British Skin Foundation (BSF)

www.britishskinfoundation.org.uk
Tel: 0207 391 6341
The British Skin Foundation (BSF) is the only UK charity dedicated to skin disease research.

Centre of Evidence Based Dermatology

www.nottingham.ac.uk/scs/divisions/evidencebaseddermatology/index.aspx
Tel: 0115 823 2434
Provides information on research into eczema.

Dermatology UK

www.dermatology.co.uk
info@dermatology.co.uk
Educational site which includes information and pictures of eczema and other skin conditions.

Eczema.com (a US site)

www.eczema.com/about-us/
Eczema.com was created to provide you with the information, tools and advice to help you understand and cope with and/or heal your eczema.

National Eczema Society

www.eczema.org
Helpline: 0800 0891122
The UK's leading eczema patient support organisation, offering help and information to everyone affected by eczema.

Nottingham Eczema Support Group

www.nottinghameczema.org.uk
Has a profusion of useful practical information, many of which are now available on podcast.

Skincare World

www.skincareworld.co.uk
An educational site for atopic eczema sufferers, their carers and healthcare professionals. A fun and informative site.

Talk Eczema

www.talkeczema.com
Offers a patient information service and forum to help eczema sufferers and their families cope with the day-to-day misery of living with eczema and dry skin conditions.

The British Association of Dermatologists

Willan House, 4 Fitzroy Square, London, W1T 5HQ
Tel: 0207-383-0266
Fax: 0207-388-5263
admin@bad.org.uk
www.bad.org.uk
The professional organisation for dermatologists in the UK and Eire.

References

Journals

Colin R Simpson, John Newton, Julia Hippisley-Cox, Aziz Sheikh, Trends in the epidemiology and prescribing of medication for eczema in England Journal of the Royal Society of Medicine JRSM > Volume 102, Number 3 > Pp. 108-117

Eczema in Early Childhood May Influence Mental Health Later ScienceDaily (Feb. 10, 2010)

Eczema Still On the Increase Across The Globe, ScienceDaily (Jan. 8, 2008) Alan D Irvine, Fleshing Out Filaggrin Phenotypes, Journal of Investigative Dermatology (2007) 127, 504-507.

Long CC, Finlay AY; The finger-tip unit--a new practical measure. Clin Exp Dermatol. 1991 Nov.) (BMJ, NOV 1989; 299: 1259-60).

Charlene Laino WebMD Health News Eczema, Peanut Allergy May Be Linked Medscape Medical News from the: American Academy of Allergy, Asthma and Immunology (AAAAI) 2010 Annual Meeting

Strachan DP. BMJ. 1989 Nov 18;299(6710):1259-60, Hay fever, hygiene, and household size.

'Atopic eczema in children management of atopic eczema in children from birth up to the age of 12 years' National Collaborating Centre for Women's and Children's Health, Commissioned by the National Institute for Health and Clinical Excellence December 2007 http://guidance.nice.org.uk/CG57.

Chronic Illness in Children its impact on Child and Family, Georgia Travis 1976 Stanford University Press.

Pediatric Infectious Disease Journal. 2008;27(6):551-552. 2008 Eczema and Infection Patricia A. Treadwell, MD.

Ong PY et al. "Endogenous antimicrobial peptides and skin infections in atopic dermatitis." New England Journal of Medicine. 2002. October 10;347(15):1151-60.) www.medicalnewstoday.com/articles/

Book List

Your Guide to Eczema
By Dr Sarah Wakelin, Hodder Arnold 2005

Eczema Free for Life
By Adnan Nasir and Priscilla Burgess, Harper, 2005

Eczema The Treatments and Therapies That Really Work
By Carolyn Charman and Sandra Lawton, Robinson, 2006

The Eczema Solution
By Sue Armstrong Brown, Vermilion, 2002

Need - 2 - Know

CENTRAL 3/6/11 Available Titles Include ...

Allergies A Parent's Guide
ISBN 978-1-86144-064-8 £8.99

Autism A Parent's Guide
ISBN 978-1-86144-069-3 £8.99

Blood Pressure The Essential Guide
ISBN 978-1-86144-067-9 £8.99

Dyslexia and Other Learning Difficulties
A Parent's Guide ISBN 978-1-86144-042-6 £8.99

Bullying A Parent's Guide
ISBN 978-1-86144-044-0 £8.99

Epilepsy The Essential Guide
ISBN 978-1-86144-063-1 £8.99

Your First Pregnancy The Essential Guide
ISBN 978-1-86144-066-2 £8.99

Gap Years The Essential Guide
ISBN 978-1-86144-079-2 £8.99

Secondary School A Parent's Guide
ISBN 978-1-86144-093-8 £9.99

Primary School A Parent's Guide
ISBN 978-1-86144-088-4 £9.99

Applying to University The Essential Guide
ISBN 978-1-86144-052-5 £8.99

ADHD The Essential Guide
ISBN 978-1-86144-060-0 £8.99

Student Cookbook – Healthy Eating The Essential Guide
ISBN 978-1-86144-069-3 £8.99

Multiple Sclerosis The Essential Guide
ISBN 978-1-86144-086-0 £8.99

Coeliac Disease The Essential Guide
ISBN 978-1-86144-087-7 £9.99

Special Educational Needs A Parent's Guide
ISBN 978-1-86144-116-4 £9.99

The Pill An Essential Guide
ISBN 978-1-86144-058-7 £8.99

University A Survival Guide
ISBN 978-1-86144-072-3 £8.99

View the full range at **www.need2knowbooks.co.uk**.
To order our titles call **01733 898103**, email **sales@n2kbooks.com** or visit the website. Selected ebooks available online.

Need - 2 - Know, Remus House, Coltsfoot Drive, Peterborough, PE2 9BF